406: Officer Needs Assistance

Memoirs of a San Francisco Police Officer

Raymond Petersen

Published by BookLocker.com, Inc., Bradenton, Florida, U.S.A.

Printed on acid-free paper.

BookLocker.com, Inc.
2015

First Edition

Dedication

To Priscilla, my beautiful wife and best friend.

To my supportive and loving family.

To my friends, who are like family.

To all the brave men and women who devote their lives to secure our safety.

Special Tribute

Raymond J. O'Brien

"Uncle Ray"

This book is also dedicated to my childhood hero, my Uncle Ray (1896–1970), Retired Inspector, San Francisco Police Department, Badge #35.

Contents

Foreword

I have known Ray Petersen for approximately fifty years. Whenever we get together, Ray and I talk fondly of the old days in the San Francisco Police Department. I was a cop in another department in Marin County before coming to the SFPD. But I was "born and raised"—as the natives say—in The City, as was Ray. I also graduated from the much-maligned Mission High School, a school mentioned in this book. You had to be assertive to survive at that school; a few classmates did end up in "the joint."

Ray and I never worked together in the police department, as he and I had different career paths. Ray's experience was much more varied than mine. He worked in many district stations, and also in the Accident Investigation Bureau. I worked in only one district station and then was sent downtown to the Hall of Justice, where for the most part I spent the rest of my career as an inspector (detective). But I served five years on patrol in Marin County before transferring to San Francisco.

While in the SFPD, I continued my education and—after obtaining AA and BA degrees in the Administration of Justice—went to graduate school and obtained a Masters and a Doctorate in Counseling Psychology.

While still in the police department, I began teaching as an adjunct professor at a local community college and at a private university in San Francisco. After retiring from the San Francisco Police Department, I began teaching full time at Palomar College in Southern California, where I still am.

My rationale in pursuing psychology as a major was simple: Since I was a cop and dealing with people and their behavior on a daily basis, I should know something about them. I began with the idea of studying the criminal mind, but as I progressed I switched and decided cops were a lot more interesting.

On my last visit to Nashville to visit Ray, we spent a few days discussing his idea for this book. I looked at some of his notes and part of his manuscript, and thought the topic very interesting and much in line with what I have been concerned with. *406: Officer Needs Assistance* covers topics I discuss with my students and with other law enforcement professionals on a daily basis.

As the title of Ray's book suggests, officers sometimes do need help dealing with the things they see and handle every day. Cops see things the average person can't even fathom. They encounter dead kids; spousal abuse; accident victims; victims of rape and murder; elderly people who have been bilked out of their life savings; homeless people who have died in the street; runaway and throw-away kids who live in doorways, huddling together for warmth; prostitutes who are victims of their pimps and sometimes their clients—and much more. In short, they experience what someone called "man's inhumanity to man." And while they are doing this police work, they are not allowed the luxury of having emotions. Cops, while working, cannot be sad, glad, angry, happy, or frustrated. They are instructed to handle their various assignments and not acknowledge their emotions. They are to treat people humanely, without being human. Then they are expected to return home and resume a "normal life," carrying on as parents, spouses, lovers, and friends.

I feel Ray touches on all these topics in his book.

At the end of a couple of chapters, Ray mentions that he felt that certain occurrences facilitated his ultimately submitting his resignation. The loss of his best friend in high school was the first disappointment. Another was the visit to Mission High and the realization that he would be dealing with kids—many about his age—who have lost their direction. When dealing with a case of spousal abuse at the Pacific Heights home of a wealthy person, Ray learned "cops see even the best people at their worst."

Juvenile court referees and other soft-on-crime professionals who sided with delinquent kids were also a source of frustration for Ray, and they contributed strongly to his ultimate decision to resign. There were other contributing factors, too. Among them:

- The sense of impotence and disappointment at not being able to extricate a victim of spousal abuse because the victim was financially dependent on the perpetrator;
- The frustration and anger one felt towards a system that returns severely neglected kids to their irresponsible family;
- Seeing a young person decapitated in an automobile accident;
- The loss of a fellow police officer and his wife in an auto accident;
- The suicide of a police officer who was Ray's colleague and friend;
- The intense pressure of always having to be on your toes and aware of any potential danger that may be coming your way.

All these things—and a multitude of other factors—can have a profound effect on a human being. But when Ray was a police officer, there was no one to talk to when you, as an officer, felt disturbed about what you were observing or doing. Officers were not supposed to *have* problems; they were supposed to *solve* problems. Thankfully, that has changed today and there is a more general acceptance of "officer needs assistance."

-- Dr. Morgan Peterson
Professor
Administration of Justice
Palomar College

Prologue

In the San Francisco Bay Area, the code "406" is a policeman's urgent radio-call for help. This help is all-too-often necessary on the streets during working hours, but also is much needed *after* hours.

In fact, help can be needed for a lifetime.

I can personally attest to that.

The following police stories are true-life events as I remember them. Many changes have occurred since my nine years as a San Francisco police officer. New laws, new political awareness, and new social attitudes have altered the American landscape—including my home town of San Francisco.

But some things remain real and compelling. And while looking back and pulling details from my memory bank, I came to realize—more than ever—the full meaning and reality of "406: Officer Needs Assistance."

Bringing these stories to the page brought me my share of flashbacks and actual anxiety attacks. Yes, some of these symptoms could be explained by my ongoing battle with Parkinson's disease. But, more than that, many memories and feelings simply have never left me.

My final story here is entitled "Complacency: Time to Hang It Up." But I never really did. Emotions and memories from those years have haunted me for decades, and will haunt me for the rest of my life.

I always wanted to stay connected with the men and women in blue. My 30-plus years in the insurance industry—in the decades after I left the San Francisco police force—often were filled with helping police men and women plan for their future and the future of their families.

After moving to my new home in Brentwood Tennessee, I promptly became involved with the Williamson County Crime Stoppers organization, as a result of which I made many new acquaintances who also had an affinity for police officers and their work.

One young man—whom I was asked to counsel—was in the throes of anxiety and panic over his upcoming retirement from the Brentwood, Tennessee Police Department. His story was troubling on many levels: he couldn't face the thought of retiring to civilian life, believing his life was over. And he facilitated that by "eating his gun"—committing suicide—in his police car. I still have the raw, heartfelt letter he wrote to me after reading rough drafts of the stories you are about to read.

All of this deepened my sense of "406: Officer Needs Assistance."

All of it left me wondering: *Where do I go from here?*

EARLY DAYS
ON THE POLICE FORCE

Chapter One
The Excelsior District

I started life as a shy kid in San Francisco, living in cramped quarters with my mother, father, grandmother, older brother, and uncle—all in a one-bathroom, 1000-square-foot house on London Street in the Excelsior District.

This neighborhood—which then was largely a mix of Italian-, Asian-, and Irish-Americans—is in the extreme southeast corner of San Francisco. Like the rest of the city, it is usually blanketed by year-round damp, cold, gray fog.

Back then, many families never ventured away from the confines of the Excelsior. Or if they did it was, as my family used to say, "to take their last trip to Colma." (Colma is known as "the graveyard capital of the U.S.," with cemeteries taking up 75 percent of its 2.2 square miles. It is located just five miles from the Excelsior District.)

Living as we did in such close quarters, families tended to fold into one another. Mothers and grandmothers often were looked to for advice and companionship. I spent many afternoons as a young boy standing on a cold, damp, drizzly street corner listening to the matrons of the block—including my own mother and grandmother—attempting to solve life's challenges for themselves and others.

Over the years, many people have asked me, "When did you first decide to become a cop?" For me, that's an easy one to answer. It happened when I was all of six years old—and it had everything to do with my Uncle Ray.

Uncle Ray was, quite simply, *different*. He was a San Francisco Police Inspector. He wore a dark blue uniform with a large, shiny star on his shirt. When he finished his shift, he would come home and regale us with "cop stories"—his adventures on the job, characters he met, tales of the dangerous and exciting hours he spent protecting the citizens of San Francisco. We would all sit around our yellow and chrome Virtue kitchen table, huddled together, listening to Uncle Ray spin his stories.

Other men I knew—including my father, the butcher, whom I dearly loved—were hard-working, salt-of-the-earth people. They were great; the backbone of America.

But they weren't glamorous. What they did for a living wasn't *colorful* and *exciting*.

And what Uncle Ray did—at least to me—*was*.

He was my knight in shining armor. He was my inspiration. He was the reason I knew *exactly* what I wanted to be when I grew up. I lived in a kid's fantasy world around him.

I was *hooked*.

* * *

In 1958, I was just twenty years old, newly married to the former Priscilla Parodi, and expecting our first child. From my freshman year at St. Ignatius High School, I had worked for my father as a butcher. In those days, there were still neighborhood markets where someone could order special cuts of meat. These markets were called "conventional markets," and were a dying breed, with the supermarkets on the way.

According to my father, I had the makings of a first-rate butcher. I agreed with him. My father really knew his craft and, fortunately for me, was happy to teach me from the ground up. But there was one huge problem.

In his opinion, the "conventional market"—where butchers like him had worked for generations—soon would be a fond memory. And where would that leave his twenty-year-old son, soon to be a father himself? Each day it gnawed at me. I knew I had to think about the future. I knew I needed to find more than being a meat-cutter.

As fate would have it, several of our most regular customers were police officers. In fact, we were so friendly with so many police officers, that many of them had attended our wedding. And more than once I heard from them, "You know, Ray, you'd make a damn fine cop. You've got the personality and the smarts for it. You really oughta think about it."

And think I did. As a matter of fact, I thought the same thing they did—that I could be a good cop. To me, this was not some hair-brained idea, not some pie-in-the-sky fantasy. Thanks to Uncle Ray, I saw this was a real, honest-to-God thing you could do with your life. And though Uncle Ray never encouraged me to become a cop, he never discouraged me either.

One Saturday, out of the blue (no pun intended), Lt. Alvin Nicolini came into our butcher shop to pick up his meat order. Lt. Nicolini was a big, gregarious man, very well-liked and an all-around nice guy. He was assigned to the Police Academy located in Golden Gate Park, and lived within a block or two of my father's butcher shop. On a regular basis, I'd deliver meats in the neighborhood for my father, and Lt. Nicolini's family sometimes was on that route.

After we exchanged a few pleasantries, Lt. Nicolini got down to the real reason he'd come in the store.

"Ray," he said, "have you done anything about the police department? I've told you in the past I think you'd be a damn fine police officer. And I've got a feeling you might agree with me on that one."

He scrutinized my face and then continued. "The city and the County of San Francisco's got a recruitment drive on to fill several vacancies within the police department. The deadline to apply is about two months away. So you think about it, Ray. I'm leaving this information here for you. Call my office if you're interested."

Still being a bit shy—and not wanting to ruffle my father's feathers—I didn't say much in response. But inside I was thanking Lt. Nicolini big-time.

And shortly thereafter I let Lt. Nicolini know that yes, I was *absolutely* interested.

In those days, the requirements to apply to take the exam were very strict. You had to be a certain height and weight, and had to have specific educational qualifications. And you had to become a resident of San Francisco, if and when you passed the exam.

This was really important to me—huge—so I went down to the civil service offices and picked up, in person, a complete information kit, including all the details. But I discussed my decision to apply with no one except my wife Priscilla. And she became my trainer.

Physical fitness was a major factor in the acceptance process. There were several physical criteria you had to meet, included height, weight, hearing, and vision. And the athletic test you had to meet—running, weight-lifting, pull-ups, and the like—were all time-sensitive. Being young and in good health was helpful, but I still had to train; there would be no second chances. You had one chance and one chance only—and failure in any of the categories meant automatic disqualification.

So my laser-sharp focus became: *pass the tests*. Almost every evening, Priscilla and I would go out to Golden Gate Park. I would run and Priscilla would time me. Luckily, I was pretty fast back then; after the intensive training, I was able to run the 100-yard dash in the 10.2 to 10.75 seconds range. I did the strength training at home in the garage, with a mixed set of dumbbells.

The knowledge portion of the test was substantial and very rigorous. There was a coaching school run by a retired Deputy Chief of Police, which specialized in test-taking for civil service jobs. Classes were held twice a week for up to eight weeks. So Priscilla and I had an extremely busy schedule. Both of us worked and, in our spare time, we managed to "Get Ray Ready" for the all-important exam day.

After weeks of training, exam day finally came. The exam would be held at the City Hall at Van Ness and Golden Gate. It was on Saturday to accommodate most applicants' work schedule. Needless to say, I was very nervous the morning of the exam, even though I was confident I was prepared.

Upon arrival at the City Hall, I saw a long line of people—men and women—waiting to enter the hall. I heard later there were more than 5,000 applicants, and 1,280 who actually sat for the written test, which was Phase One. If you made it past Phase One, you then had to pass the agility portion, the health screening, and, of course, the background check. In those days, having received a traffic ticket with a fine greater than $50 could be sufficient reason to get you eliminated.

After going through the entire testing process, the Civil Service Commission posted the final result of the testing.

And I was stunned.

In a good way.

As I looked at the results on the Commission wall, I saw my name in 20th position.

Way, way higher than I would have dreamed.

And I had not benefited from the 20-point credit given to military veterans. That meant I *actually* placed in the Top 10 out of 5,000-plus original applicants.

I was on my way.

Chapter Two
Police Academy

Several days passed and I received notice from the Civil Service Commission that I was to appear at the Hall of Justice for the swearing-in ceremony, for what was to be the 87th Recruit Class. It was with mixed emotion that I gave notice to my employer—my father—that I was embarking on a new career path. Overall, my family was very happy for me, especially Priscilla, although we had no idea the toll this road would demand.

I took two or three weeks to prepare for my new life. This included keeping up with my work-out routine, continuing to work in my father's butcher shop, and visiting with family and friends.

During this time, one thing I was told by some of the "customer cops" at the butcher shop was disquieting.

"You'll lose some of your so-called friends," they told me. "Even friends from way back. Some folks *just don't like cops*—that's all there is to it."

I held my tongue when they said that, thinking, *Well, I doubt I'll have that problem.*

Almost immediately, I was proven wrong.

About a week before the swearing-in ceremony, I went to the home of one of my closest friends. He wasn't there—he had been at school "back east" for a couple of years—but his mom and dad were there, and they invited me into their living room. I had known them for several years, and they were always very nice and hospitable to me. Priscilla and I considered them like family. I felt very comfortable sharing my good news with them.

"Mr. and Mrs. _____, I want you to be among the first to know I passed the entrance exam to become a police officer," I said. "I join the police force next week."

I wasn't prepared for what happened next.

Immediately, the room became deadly quiet. The atmosphere turned cold and hostile.

After what seemed an eternity, Mr. _____ looked up and said to me very sarcastically, "So you're going to be one of those bums on the take."

I don't clearly remember what happened after that. But I know I quickly left their house, no longer feeling welcome. As I walked away, I felt a lump rise in my throat.

What just happened? I wondered. *Is this what I was warned about?*

Fast-forward to several months later.

After I'd somewhat forgotten that awkward scene with his parents, my friend sent an invitation to Priscilla and me to a reception at his parents' house. He and his new wife were coming from the east coast to San Francisco for a visit, and Priscilla and I were eager to see them. By this time, I hadn't seen my friend in more than two years.

But when I finally did, something very strange happened.

Priscilla and I rang the doorbell and waited to be let it. When my friend answered the door, he was noticeably taken aback to see Priscilla and me. He was normally a hug-you, pat-you-on-the-back, super-friendly type of guy. But he certainly wasn't now. I immediately felt the same cold draft I had experienced when I went to his parents' house several months before.

The tension mounted as Priscilla and I walked into the party. It became so awkward and uncomfortable I finally took my friend aside and asked, "What's wrong, _____ ? You've acted cold toward Priscilla and me all evening."

I will never forget his response.

"You and I have nothing in common anymore," he said coldly.

And that was pretty much it, as far as he was concerned. Evidently, his view was, *Soon I'll graduate from an Ivy League school. But Ray is just a cop. We have nothing in common.*

That was the last time I ever spoke to my long-time friend. He never sent me another invitation, and I never saw him again. I'd become a cop, and—in his mind—that meant he should never again have anything to do with me.

That was the first of many such reactions to my new job.

The day of the swearing-in ceremony finally arrived. The ceremony was to take place at the Hall of Justice near historic Chinatown. The official day and time was Friday at 10 a.m.

Priscilla and I, along with the other thirty-five recruits and their families, gathered in the huge rotunda of the Hall of Justice. Chief of Police Tom Cahill was on hand to administer the oath of office. Welcoming remarks were made from some of the police commissioners, representatives from City Hall and, of course, Chief Cahill, whose thick Irish brogue made it difficult to understand what he was saying.

The moment that was to change my life was at hand.

"Recruits, please raise your right hand and face the colors," intoned Chief Cahill.

Upon finishing the oath, Chief Cahill faced the audience and said, "Ladies and gentlemen . . . It is with great pride that I introduce you to the 87th recruit class for the City and County of San Francisco." People erupted in cheers, applause, tears of joy, and expressions of good wishes.

And I just stood there beaming, with one thought running endlessly through my mind:

Wow . . . Now I'm a San Francisco police officer.

Chapter Three
Cadet Training

Sgt. Ed Eppting, the instructor assigned to the police academy, called the 87th recruit class to order. Sgt. Eppting proceeded to give us an overview of what was to take place over the next few hours and days. He told us we were expected to have our basic equipment and academy uniform by the time we started class the following Monday at 8 a.m.

Although it seems strange today, in 1959 the City of San Francisco did not feel it had the budget to provide necessary gear to its police officers. So each recruit was fully responsible for the costs of getting outfitted—including his or her gun or guns, badge (referred to as the "star" or "buzzer,") call-box key, bullets, whistle, handcuffs, and nightstick.

The announcement by Sgt. Eppting that we had to buy our own police equipment made for an amusing moment—or one that's amusing now. We all looked at each other with an expression that said, *How do we pay for all this stuff?"*

Without missing a beat, Sgt Eppting advised us that members of the San Francisco Police Credit Union would be on hand, to arrange loans so each of us could pay for our necessities.

Welcome to the world of credit, I thought. Prior to this, I'd paid for everything in my entire life with cash or a check. But now I had a new, "secure" job—and promptly was several hundred dollars in debt. (And remember that in 1959 several hundred dollars was the salary you'd likely earn over a month or two.)

So the "credit thing" was a bit disquieting. But, to me, there was something much worse. That afternoon there were more than thirty cadets suddenly carrying weapons. And how much training had many of us received on the proper use of a firearm?

Precisely none.

So now you had thirty (mostly untrained) cadets. Each with a gun. And six bullets. Over the entire weekend.

Quite a scary scenario.

I soon got outfitted, and headed home a very happy and proud fellow. Priscilla and I made a party of it, celebrating the entire weekend with family and friends. We were expecting our first child and—despite some "friends" not being able to handle my becoming a police officer—things were looking up.

My dream had crystallized. And it would become more real Monday morning at 8 a.m.

* * *

The police academy was located near Golden Gate Park on Fulton Street. The building was very old but well-maintained. We were greeted by the staff, and then class was called to order. Since San Francisco was one of a handful of police departments in the bay area that had an actual training program, there were cadets from other departments included in our class. These men were assigned to the academy to satisfy their department's requirements.

The staff spent the first day outlining what we should expect over the next fourteen weeks. We were told that, in addition to the academy instructors, there would be several guest speakers addressing special subjects. We also learned not all classes would take place at the Fulton Street location; there would be "field trips," as well. These would be actual patrol duties, in which we would work with an experienced officer in a way similar to what is known in many police departments as a "ride-along" program.

Most "ride-along" programs were designed for select citizens (for example, from the San Francisco Emergency Association), who would ride along with police officers to gain a deeper understanding of what the officers did. It was a public education program and—to a degree—a PR program, because one of its intents was to cultivate better relationships between cops, local organizations, and the community.

The difference between our program and a standard "ride-along" program was ours was for cadet cops and was *very real.* As we rode with the experienced officer, we would wear our uniform, a gun, and "star" (badge). We also would have the power of arrest.

Before I knew it, it was 5 p.m. and the end of a very exciting first day. I could hardly wait to get home to Priscilla, to tell her all about Day One. Also, I would need to explain to her why—from this day forward—I would always have to include a gun as part of my attire whenever I left the house. The reason was clear and straightforward: In California at that time, a police officer was expected to be technically on duty twenty-four hours a day, seven days a week. For example, if you were off-duty and happened to walk in on a robbery in progress, it was your sworn duty to size-up the situation and take appropriate action. As time went by and I gained more and more experience, I gained a deeper sense of what "appropriate action" meant.

After the first day or so, I began learning who my classmates were, and details about their lives. As it turns out, I was the youngest of the group. The age range was from twenty-one to mid-thirties. Most cadets were married and all were male. And there was a wide variety of (previous) occupations represented: teachers, military police, assorted white collar professionals, a fireman, and, of course, one butcher.

From the very first day, we were lectured about conducting ourselves as professionals. These behavioral demands were strict, and ultimately some cadets would "wash out" of the class because they could not avoid trouble. Others resigned or were asked to resign—including one for committing arson at a very prominent eatery. The awesome responsibility of wearing "the buzzer" (badge) was too much for some to handle. And—before our careers eventually ended—*all* of us in the 87th class would feel the awesome weight of the buzzer. (The badge was referred to as "the buzzer" because your badge—like the buzzer in an apartment building—allowed you to gain access pretty much anywhere.)

As classes continued, Sgt. Eppting outlined the calendar of events for the next fourteen weeks, leading up to our graduation. A significant part of that training would involve learning city, state, and federal law. Self-defense training was also extremely important; we needed to know how to defend ourselves in street fights, or from common drunks, juveniles, mental patients, or anyone else resisting arrest.

Sgt. Eppting assigned partners to work out together. Part of the work-out involved boxing. Luckily, I had some experience with this because I'd boxed in Golden Gloves tournaments. But this was very different. This was a completely different level. Now the "prize" for learning to box was the ability to avoid serious injury or even death. So everyone took it extremely seriously, and, as a result, it was very intense.

My work-out and boxing partner was Willie Frazier, one of a handful of African-American officers on the San Francisco police force at that time. Willie was one of the older cadets, around thirty years of age, married with four or five children. He was a great guy—kind, good-looking, athletic, and very sharp—and ultimately wound up as an aid to the Police Commission, assigned to the Chief's office. This was during a time when African-Americans were extremely underrepresented on the San Francisco police force—there were barely ten black cops in the city—and the force knew it had to appoint more highly qualified African-Americans to higher-level positions. Willie was perfect for that.

But before that happened, I had to spar with Willie and—I'm here to tell you—he packed one hell of a punch! Several times Willie caught me with left hooks or right jabs, and I swear I could hear bells ringing! But at least I could take a punch. And in time this training would come in very handy.

Chapter Four
First Assignment

At this time—the late 1950s—San Francisco was first experiencing the civil disorder that would explode across America in the 1960s. Along with often-violent para-military groups such as the Black Panthers and Weathermen, street gangs were present and flourishing. Later, New York, Los Angeles, Chicago, and other major cities would become known as centers of gang activity, but back then San Francisco was seemingly leading the way. A lot of gang activity was directly related to racial tension—which also would explode dramatically in the 1960s. Many neighborhoods were mixed-race and you had a lot of the tension that went along with that.

You also had a situation in which members of various ethnic groups took pride in not cooperating with the police. Or refused to cooperate because they feared for their status or safety. For example, a member of the Chinese community might be ostracized—or worse—if he was seen as cooperating with the police. This led to a tense, edgy, dangerous atmosphere for cops and citizens around San Francisco. We were trained to deal with violent criminals, violent or non-violent mentally ill people, even people literally spitting in our faces. And we had to deal with people intentionally trying to "ring our bells" by doing things such as blocking public property or otherwise engaging in civil disobedience, directed at "the Establishment," of which cops were the public face. We often felt like we were at war with the community—even as we did everything in our power to keep it safe and orderly.

* * *

The power of the "buzzer" is awesome and the responsibility that goes with it could be devastating. We had fourteen weeks to learn hundreds of codes designed to enforce the law. It was expected that an officer would know exactly what he or she can and cannot legally do under various circumstances. As I found out when I was sent out on patrol, a police officer frequently has a split-second to make a decision that could affect several people for the rest of their lives. In some cases, your decision might even save or end someone's life.

It certainly was a stressful system to be part of. As a police officer, you had to interface with the victim and/or perpetrator and do your best to bring someone to justice. Then, an attorney would get the case—after the fact, with weeks, months, or years in which to review it—and present it to twelve strangers who had nothing to do with the incident, but who were expected to pass judgment. In those instances in which an officer may have made a mistake, he's held accountable and his career may be at stake. Great!

At the time, it seemed like we were buried in codes. But we had to learn them, had to be completely on top of them. A basic knowledge of the codes provided us valuable tools with which to practice our profession. In fact, there were sections in the municipal code that were more enforceable than the state's penal code.

Sometimes we would make an arrest using a variety of codes, knowing at least one of them would "stick." Part of our education involved working with the District Attorney's office to learn how to present a case for prosecution. This is an ongoing process, day-in and day-out. Any error could result in a criminal being released back into society to continue causing problems.

As I mentioned earlier, part of our training included actually going out into the field one night or day a week, in uniform. Generally this would be on a Friday, as Fridays typically brought about more action, thus more learning opportunities for us rookie cops. We would receive our assignments on Thursday, then on Friday go to wherever we were assigned, rather than to the academy.

My first assignment was the Juvenile Bureau. The office was located on Greenwich Street in the Marina neighborhood. From the outside, it looked like a branch library, but once inside that resemblance ended. As I got there and looked around, my eyes took in wanted posters, bulletins covering lost children, and photos of suspected gang members. There was a display case containing various types of weapons such as knives, switchblades, guns (zip guns), clubs, brass knuckles, lead pipes, and swords. All these weapons had been taken from juveniles during an arrest. As I learned later in the evening, many of the weapons were even taken from students during school hours.

That night my tour of duty was 4 p.m. to 12 a.m. and I was in plain clothes—no uniform—which was the dress code for the Juvenile Bureau. The officer I was assigned to for the first night was Inspector George Emil, who, years later, became Chief of Police.

"We'll be on patrol tonight in an unmarked car," George said to me, after we shook hands. "We'll be following up on cases I've been assigned. We'll also be available to handle anything juvenile-related that may happen."

Our call number for the evening was Juvenile 3. George gave me a once-over on how to use the police radio and I became very anxious. I was intensely aware of the seriousness and importance of this duty. My job was to listen for our call sign and then acknowledge receipt. It would go something like "From dispatch . . . Juvenile 3, response Juvenile 3 . . . dispatch – Juvenile 3 . . . a 418 (fight) at Marina Junior High . . . Northern 4 (station car) is responding . . . response Juvenile 3, 10-4."

We started the shift with a trip to the drive-in for a cup of coffee. Above his steaming cup, George looked over at me and said, "We'll be serving subpoenas tonight and interviewing witnesses in preparation for court cases. We'll also be checking out places known to be gang hangouts. All along, we have to be available for any calls from dispatch."

After we finished our coffee, George said, "Okay . . . let's run over to Mission High School. We need to talk with one of the teachers regarding a possible drug problem there."

Mission High was the neighborhood high school for the Mission and Upper Market sections of the city. This was a very rough, very dangerous section of the city, with a large Mexican-American and African-American population. It had a reputation of being a prep school for future attendees of San Quentin Prison, just across the bay from San Francisco's Mission District.

As he briefed me, George looked me straight in the eye, a serious expression on his face. "This high school is integrated—a mix of Mexican, Asian, black, and white students," he said. "It's a cauldron of youthful energy and unrest. And it's a breeding ground for drug dealers who want to recruit 'soldiers' to carry out their dirty work."

When we got to the school, the teacher we spoke with echoed George's concerns.

"Unfortunately, your impression of the school is exactly right," he said. "I often fear for my own safety, along with the safety of other staff members and the student body."

I listened in disbelief as this experienced teacher told us what an average day at the school was like. After listening for about an hour, I went away shaking my head. *When did it come to pass that students are now running schools?*, I wondered.

"You think that's awful, Ray? Well you're right," George said as we drove away from Mission High. "But what's worse is, that's just a quick peek under the blanket of what you have to look forward to."

As time went by, I gained a deeper and deeper understanding of what George meant by that remark. This was many years before shootings on campuses became commonplace. But the situation in some of our high schools already was alarming.

The rest of the evening was spent responding to calls suspected of being juvenile-related. We also served warrants on kids suspected of prior offenses.

We returned to the Juvenile Bureau to review our tour of duty and to catch up on any required paperwork. At about 11:45 p.m., George said we would knock off; our watch was over.

On my way home, I reflected on my first "on duty" night on the street. It hit me that I was not much older than some of the kids we'd encountered that night. I was twenty-one and the Juvenile Bureau handled kids up to eighteen years of age. It gave me a very funny feeling.

And there was something else: My wife Priscilla and I now were expecting our first child. What kind of world would our child grow up in? What kind of parents would we be? I was beginning to see young people and families hit hard by life or by their own poor decisions. And even cop families are not immune from those things.

Chapter Five
Shark Attack

As part of our fourteen-week training curriculum, we listened to many visiting instructors lecture on their specialties. Such was the case when we met a colorful, impressive police officer from Australia. He was touring various cities in the United States, accumulating information that might prove helpful to his own department as they planned an overhaul.

It was very interesting to hear how the officer's Australian jurisdiction dealt with the same issues we were being trained to handle. One—believe it or not—was the ongoing threat of shark attacks. As the Australian cop spoke to us, this topic was particularly timely because a young man had recently lost his life in a shark attack at Bakers Beach, right outside of San Francisco. I had seen the grisly photos of this victim in the coroner's office. The shark's first bite had resulted in the man losing everything from his right shoulder to his hip.

The Australian officer told us shark attacks were a common occurrence in his native country. In fact, an attack had taken the life of a daughter of one of his fellow officers. Speaking in his thick Aussie accent, he told us the shocking, true-life story:

"My friend—and fellow officer—was picnicking with his wife and two children on one of the many beaches near where they lived," the officer began. "My friend's wife wanted to take a picture of her two children playing in the water. The water was no deeper than a foot—completely safe, one would think.

"Suddenly—as my friend's wife attempted to take the photo—a huge shark came up on its side, grabbed her little girl, and swam off . . . never to be seen again. The little girl's body was never recovered."

As we all say there, stunned, as the officer concluded his story.

"There is a crucial lesson in this story, which you must never forget: Never, ever take your safety in the water for granted."

Chapter Six
Do You Kiss on the First Date?

Part of our Police Academy training included Friday night fieldwork. Instead of class work, we recruits were assigned to various locations to work with veteran police officers to get hands-on experience.

One particular Friday night, I was assigned to the Bureau of Special Services (BSS). The BSS was a plainclothes-unit within the Inspectors Bureau. It included "vice" as part of its function, an "umbrella term" covering such things as alcohol- or narcotics-related crimes, theft, assault, or murder. (Originally, the BSS had been known as "The Vice Squad.") Another recruit, Bill Schmidt, and I were told to be at the Hall of Justice at 7 p.m. wearing street clothes. I arrived wearing a sports coat, a tie, and a pair of slacks—probably looking like a college freshman. Bill was similarly dressed.

As we walked in, Fred Mullins—a very friendly Irish sergeant—greeted us. Fred took one look at us, laughed loudly, and said, "Both of you go home and change out of those duds. Change into something shabby and dirty. If your clothes are stained or have paint all over them, all the better. Trust me—you're not going to a classy place tonight."

As Bill and I exchanged baffled looks, Fred said, "Go on now . . . but report back to my office at 10 p.m." No further explanation was given.

At precisely 10 p.m., the shabby version of Bill and I stood in front of Sgt. Mullins. After giving us the once-over, the sergeant nodded his approval. Then he and his police partner, Jim Casey, told us to take a seat so they could fill us in on the assignment.

During this time—the late fifties—San Francisco was going through the "counter-culture" Beatnik era, which later would explode into the Flower Power decade of the sixties. There were

406: Officer Needs Assistance

gay bars around, but they were not yet out in the open. Also at this time, the city began to experience the growth of "after-hours clubs." These establishments opened their doors at 2 a.m., because the curfew for bars was 2 a.m. These "after-hours clubs" were not allowed to sell liquor, nor did they have a license to do so. What they *did* dish up was food, entertainment, soft drinks—and a place for the underworld to congregate.

Needless to say, various law enforcement agencies—the San Francisco Police Department, FBI, INS (Immigration and Naturalization Service), and ABC (Alcoholic Beverage Control)—paid a great deal of attention to these after-hours clubs. Of the various agencies, one of the most powerful was the ABC. If a place of business could be identified as a public nuisance because of its activities, the ABC could shut it down.

It was common knowledge that liquor, drugs, gambling, and questionable sexual delights were illegally available at these clubs. The trick—no pun intended—was to catch the perpetrators in some violation of the law, most often the selling of liquor. Dispensing liquor after hours and without a license was a major crime, making the after-hours club subject to a huge fine and suspension of their right to keep the doors open for business.

After giving us a thorough briefing on the nature of the after-hours clubs, Sgt. Mullins said to Bill and me, "Your objective tonight is very specific. We want you to go to a club called the Broken Drum, pretending to be a homosexual couple, and try to make a liquor buy. This club is quite notorious; it's a known hang-out for criminals."

Sgt. Mullins then showed us mug shots of several criminals known to frequent the Broken Drum, some of whom had warrants out for their arrest. "Remember—if you encounter any of these guys, they are very, very dangerous characters," he said.

Then Jim Casey spoke up. "Turn over your gun and handcuffs to me—right now—just in case the bouncer pats you down as you enter the club. But keep your star [badge]. If you're able to buy booze, you are to immediately affect an arrest."

"But understand something," Sgt. Mullins interjected. "These guys aren't going quietly. You'll probably have to fight your way out of the place. But you won't be without back-up. If you make an arrest, throw something out the window—a chair, barstool, glass, I don't care what it is—and that will alert back-up officers to rush up there and help you. They'll be watching the windows for that sign from you."

The Broken Drum was located in the second story of a building at the corner of Market Street and the Embarcadero, by the waterfront. At around 2:30 a.m., Bill and I wandered up a very narrow, dark flight of stairs to the underworld. We were greeted at the top of the landing by a no-neck pit bull of a guy, who was about three feet wide. After getting the visual once over, we were allowed past.

Inside, the atmosphere was dark and foreboding. There was hardly any light in the place; it took your eyes a long minute or two to adjust. Tables were scattered around, and a very loud band was playing. Bill and I found a seat towards the rear that allowed us to see—or see as best we could, considering we weren't bats.

It didn't take us long to see we were in an "anything goes" environment. It felt like we had walked into a movie set, and were sitting in the middle of Central Casting. The waitress came over.

"What will you boys have tonight?" she asked.

"Coffee, please," I said. Bill ordered the same.

When we got our java, we noticed all beverages were being served in a cup or mug. In this way, it would be more difficult to spot if someone near you was being served beer, wine, or liquor.

Sitting there with our coffees, Bill and I quickly saw we were the only "couple" not smooching or holding hands. (Before we'd gone into the club, I'd smirked at Bill and said, "I feel I should tell you . . . I don't go all the way on the first date. But holding hands is okay.") Looking around, I was glad Bill and I had that understanding!

After two very uncomfortable hours—during which we unsuccessfully tried to buy booze—we decided nothing was going to happen. In retrospect, that isn't particularly surprising. Bill and I probably stood out like sore thumbs. But that wasn't a bad thing, as far as we were concerned. We left at around 4:30 a.m.

After we got back to the precinct, Sgt. Mullins and Jim Casey debriefed us. At about 5 a.m., they told us the assignment was over and we could go home and get some good sleep. Bill and I were disappointed we hadn't made a bust, but were grateful for the learning experience. Oh and . . . that was our last "date."

RICHMOND STATION STORIES

Richmond Station

My first police assignment was Richmond Station, located in the middle of a block of 6th Avenue, between Geary Boulevard and Anza Street. The station was in a non-descript, 1,800-square-foot brick building, set in the middle of a Victorian, residential neighborhood, with lots of family houses on either side. As you drove past the houses, you'd often see folks sitting out on their front porches, reading the newspaper or casually talking with each other.

Parking for our police cruisers was in the back of the building. The facility also featured a holding cell and a telephone call box out on the street, a block down the sidewalk from the precinct. Inside, the building featured mug shots of criminals up on the wall and offices and cubicles for the radio car crews.

The weather in Richmond District was foggy most of the time—damp, drizzly, cold, and windy. Even when the sun shone there was a constant chill in the air. Fog would roll in so thick you could almost cut it.

The Richmond District ran all the way out to the ocean, and offered a variety of now-fondly-remembered eateries. There was Mel's Drive-In, Miz Brown's Feed Bag (where we often went for hamburgers and milkshakes), The Hickory Pit on California Street, the very popular El Sombrero Mexican restaurant, and Bill's Hamburgers out on Clement Street. On California Street in the Laurel Village area there were many upscale clothing, coffee, and housewares shops. Among the popular watering holes were O'Sheas and the Blue Danube.

Other popular institutions formed the backbone of the district. These included the old St. Ignatius High School, Lone Mountain College for Women (now part of the University of San Francisco), the University of San Francisco itself, the French Hospital, the Legion of Honor, and St. Mary's Hospital on Stanyan Street. St. Mary's was an especially important institution to our family. Most of our children were born there, and most of our older relatives died there. If a child needed his or her tonsils removed, or anyone needed virtually any medical service, we would go to St. Mary's.

The houses in the Richmond District were mostly of the stucco, built-right-next-to-each-other variety, with a small patch of lawn in front. From the inner part of the district, all the way out to the beach, all the houses seemed the same.

The busiest streets in the district were Clement, California, and Geary. Many movie theatres, grocery stores, butcher shops, catering halls, and churches lined these streets. The beautifully ornate Russian Orthodox Church was part of the neighborhood, as were many Catholic parishes. The large Jewish population worshiped in a large temple in the district, and the Jewish people also had a very busy community center.

Because the district was so heavily populated, it had a great need for schools. As a result, nearly every neighborhood offered many grade schools, junior highs, and high schools, public and private. Most of what was there in the 1960s still is there today, including, of course, Golden Gate Park, which is a large part of this district.

Butch

When I first was assigned to Richmond Station, I was disappointed I was not going to one of the high-crime stations like Central, Northern, or Mission, because I felt it would have assured a faster career-track. But I soon changed my mind about that. In fact, I discovered that, by being assigned to Richmond, I had an advantage over my classmates. Since Richmond was a slower-paced station, I was given the opportunity to experience much more, much sooner. For example, I was given solo radio-car duty after just three months—much sooner than usual. My captain said he was confident I could handle it.

One of the other "pluses" of working out of Richmond was the high level of experience of the other officers there. Richmond was nicknamed "The Farm" because it often was an officer's last assignment prior to retirement.

One of the legendary cops I met at Richmond shortly after being assigned there was Sgt. Chester Philips. Chester was a big, pot-bellied, lumbering man whose uniform looked like an old-fashioned, walking sandwich board. He had at least thirty years experience, but he had zero interest in retiring. When I asked him why, he replied, "I'm single—no wife, no kids. Retire? Are you kidding me? I wouldn't know what to do with myself." The job was his family.

Chester was reserved and, at first, a bit distant, but I grew to like him once he gave me the opportunity to know him. He began to show he trusted me.

Chester may not have had a wife or girlfriend, but he did love something very intensely. That something was alcohol. And he had no problem tending to his craving, considering the great number of bars in the Richmond district. This was especially true when we worked the midnight to 8 a.m. watch.

As a patrol sergeant, Chester was responsible for the large number of beat officers and radio car officers in his sector. He needed to know the whereabouts of each member of his crew. To accomplish this, Chester usually would request that one of the radio cars pick him up and drive him around for a couple of hours during his tour of duty. Often Chester requested that I be his designated driver. That became even more common after Chester found out that, prior to my joining the police department, I had been a butcher. From that moment on, he always called me Butch.

One night at about 2:30 a.m., I got a call from communications, telling me to meet Chester at 25th and Clement. As soon as I heard that, I knew Chester wanted to ride around for awhile—and that his desire probably was related to his large alcohol intake.

Was I ever right.

As soon as I got to Chester, I saw he was really rocking and rolling. I didn't know what he was celebrating, but he was feeling no pain. My job, basically, was to drive him around and keep him out of the way until he "felt better."

As it turns out, Chester actually lived within the district. And he suddenly turned to me—slurring his words all over the place—and said, "Hey . . . Butch . . . ya know . . . uh . . . ya know I live 'round here? Yup, sure do . . . I . . . I wanna show you my pad." He told me to drive him to his apartment.

The situation suddenly felt strange and slightly eerie, but he was Sgt. Phillips so I dutifully complied.

"Come on, Butch," he slurred as we arrived in front of his building. "Come on . . . come on up . . . come on up to my place. I got something to show ya."

Once I cleared with communications, I followed Chester up to his pad.

As soon as I entered his apartment, I immediately saw—to put it diplomatically—that it lacked a woman's touch. More to the point, it was a total disaster. Clothes and dirty dishes were stacked everywhere, and the air was stale. Entering the kitchen, I discovered what Chester did with the donuts and 19-cent hamburgers he brought home every night from the station. The kitchen windowsill "showcased" dozens of gallon-size mayonnaise jars crammed full of donuts and burgers. God only knows how long they had been there.

(A note of explanation regarding this strange sight: Each night at closing time, around midnight, the manager of Jet's Drive-In would call Richmond station and ask if a radio car in the area would come by and pick up their left-over donuts and burgers. Some of the cops would then warm the burgers by placing them on the steam radiator in the station's business office. Most nights, there were some for Chester to take home.)

Anyway . . . while we were in the kitchen, Chester slurred, "Butch . . . I . . . I . . . I want to show you something you will appreciate." With that, he suddenly pulled out a twelve-inch chef's knife. Still rocking and rolling to beat the band, he began to demonstrate his ability to sharpen knives. He shut his eyes and bragged, "There's absolutely no doubt about it, Butch. No doubt. I'm the best knife man you'll ever see."

That seemed open to debate.

But I did know one thing for certain, and I was thinking it right then: *If he misses and cuts off his fingers while in uniform, we'll never be able to explain this.*

Finally, Chester's demonstration ended, and we left his apartment. I suggested we go grab something to eat before the restaurants begin to fill up with the breakfast crowds.

By the time our tour of duty ended that night, at 8 a.m., Chester was none the worse for wear. (I couldn't claim the same.) It was hard to believe what he and I had been through that night. Thankfully, I was transferred to Central Station shortly afterwards, and never witnessed Chester's drunken knife-wielding talents again.

The "802"

I was working the midnight watch in the Richmond 4 car with my supervisor and training officer, Al Rizzo.

It was a typical San Francisco summer night in the Richmond district—foggy and cold, with harsh, damp breezes blowing in from the ocean.

Around 3 a.m., the radio broke the silence and we were dispatched to an old apartment building on 10th Avenue, just off Geary Boulevard.

"10-4 . . . on our way," Al shot back to the dispatcher, after which Communications advised us we were to meet a coroner's ambulance regarding a possible death.

Upon arrival at the scene, the deputy coroner told us it appeared we had an 802 (dead person).

"This will be a first for Officer Petersen," Al said. "He's only two weeks out of the police academy."

"Is that right?" the deputy coroner grunted. "Well, then, come with me, Petersen. Observe what I do. And take good notes for the report for the Medical Examiner's office."

I shot a glance at Al, then dutifully followed.

The deputy coroner led me to the place of death—the victim's bedroom. The dead man was an enormously fat, elderly man. It was sad to see him lying there. But what was worse was the incredible stench that permeated the room. It was obvious the poor man had been dead for several days. He was really "ripe."

The first thing we had to do was determine if this death was anything but a natural event. We checked the stove for gas leakage. Nothing. And there was no evidence of a struggle or break-in. No weapons found. The only thing we heard was the low, endless babble coming from the television in the corner of the living room.

At that point, Al jumped on the radio again.

"Confirming an 802," he called in to Communications. "Request another radio car, to help secure apartment."

37

I started to leave the bedroom, but the deputy coroner stopped me in my tracks.

"You're not finished here," he barked. "We need your help getting the 802 out of the building."

I turned back toward the dead man. A wave of relentless nausea began to wash over me.

The man's enormous body was lifted onto the gurney and secured with leather straps. Al, two coroner's deputies, and I then hoisted the gurney up over our heads, each holding a corner handle. Grunting and sweating with each step we could muster, we started inching down the stairs.

This maneuver would have been extremely difficult under the best of circumstances, but it was next-to-impossible because of the nature of the apartment building and staircase. Probably built in the early 1900s, the three-story building held six apartments, three on each side of the extremely narrow, winding outdoor staircase. To make matters worse, we could barely see where we were going.

As we heaved, grunted, cursed, and sweated our way down the staircase, the impossible occurred:

Things went from terrible to way worse.

I suddenly felt a liquid substance running down my right sleeve. *What in the name of . . .?*, I thought. Then it hit me in another nauseating wave: *Oh, my God . . . The 802's body is coming apart!* As the stinking liquid continued to ooze over my arm, the odor became almost too much to bear. Inhaling the disgusting odor, I suddenly flashed back to a past event:

Once, when I was working in my dad's butcher shop, I had cut into a rancid beef liver that exuded this same, horrible stench. I hoped I'd never smell that again. I didn't get my wish.

After what seemed like hours, we finally got the old man's body placed in the coroner's ambulance. We followed it to Park Emergency Hospital in our patrol car.

Later we had the chance to discuss the case with the deputy coroner at Park Emergency. I was still reeking the horrible odor.

"Here," he said to us, going over to his medical bag and pulling out a pale, pink liquid. "This stuff is pretty good. It should help you get the stench off your clothes and bodies."

Coincidentally, this "pale, pink liquid" was one of the products manufactured by my Uncle Frank at Eureka Fluid Works, the embalming chemical company where he had worked. It was the first time I had to use it, though—and hoped it would be my last.

Several weeks later, Al and I received autopsy details about the 802. The dead man was an 87 year-old widower who had a history of heart problems.

There were no signs of foul play.

More Than a Newspaper Boy

During my tour of duty at the Richmond Station, a series of mysterious and disquieting burglaries took place. One of the reasons they were so disturbing was where and when they took place—at heavily populated apartment buildings during *daylight* hours. And in *none* of the cases was there any sign of forced entry.

The police came to believe the burglaries were related because of the thief's m.o. But we had no leads.

One Saturday afternoon, I received a sudden call and was dispatched to an apartment complex.

"909X on 12th Avenue near Fulton Street," came the call in from the dispatcher. (A "909" indicates "interview victim" and "X" indicates female victim.)

I was working solo that afternoon. After rushing to the scene, I found myself talking to a nicely dressed, middle-aged woman, who told me she lived alone. She told me she was the person who had called the police.

"I noticed a number of small items missing," she told me. "Several pieces of jewelry. They're small but very valuable to me." She was trying to stay composed, but obviously was very distraught.

I started gently asking her a series of questions, to try to get the clearest-possible sense of her lifestyle and anything that may be pertinent to the burglary.

"If you will, please walk me through your day. What hours do you keep here at your apartment?" I asked.

"I'm gone a lot," she replied. "I leave fairly early each weekday morning for work, and almost never return before 6 p.m. But weekends—like today—I don't go out a whole lot. I'm here almost all the time."

I persisted in my questioning, trying to get a better sense of whom she might interact with each day.

After asking a number of additional questions, I turned to her and asked, "Do you get a daily newspaper left here?"

"Why, yes. Yes, I do. Several other occupants of the building do, too. "

She offered me the name of the 15-year-old *San Francisco Chronicle* delivery boy. Equally important, she told me he had a key to her and other apartments. And that he'd let himself in to deliver newspapers.

Over the next couple of weeks, I took reports from several other burglary victims in the same general area. I forwarded all information to the Burglary Detail for their follow-up.

Meanwhile, something about the newspaper-delivery boy kept whispering around in my head.

The whisper grew louder and more distinct when I learned the "big reveal" that several of the other victims *had the same newspaper boy*. I passed this along to the Burglary Detail, knowing they would pounce on it.

They did.

A short time later, the case inspector interviewed the boy. He had a real "Golden Boy" aura about him. He was from a good family, and was polite and cooperative. At first the kid pulled the, "I don't know what you're talking about" routine, but ultimately confessed to several dozen jobs he had pulled. He told the inspector he had buried the loot in Golden Gate Park, just off Fulton Street, adjacent to the crime-scene area.

Later that day, some of San Francisco's Finest found themselves at Golden Gate Park, engaged in the seemingly bizarre activity of digging up shrubs and flower beds. The effort was worth it. The cops recovered several thousand dollars worth of jewelry and other stolen items, which were eventually returned to their rightful owners. More than twenty open burglary cases thus were closed.

And for me, the story has an even happier ending:

Because of that voice in my head that had whispered *the newspaper boy . . . the newspaper boy*—and because of my follow-up on that—I was credited with the arrest. I received a Chief's Commendation for a job well done.

Better still, the suspect was taken off the street. He was tried in Juvenile Court, found guilty, and sent to the CYA (California Youth Authority) for one year, plus probation upon release.

My Car Won't Start

In early 1960, while I was stationed at Richmond Station, there were numerous reports of rapes in the outer Richmond district—most taking place in condominium complexes with open parking garages. At least ten rapes of this nature had occurred in the previous few months. The District was collectively terrified. We knew we had to get this rapist—and soon.

While patrolling in the Richmond 4 car at around 1 a.m. on a Saturday, I received a 909X ("909" means "call"; "X" refers to a call involving a female victim) at the apartment complex located at 47th Ave and LaPlaya. I sped through the streets to get there and, upon arrival, was greeted by a white, brunette female who was very distraught and disheveled. She told me she just had been sexually assaulted.

"He went that way!" she screamed hysterically. *"He went that way!"*

Through her tears and shock, she gave me her best-possible description of the suspect.

"He was black," she said (which alone was unusual; the neighborhood was lily white). "He was athletically built and dressed kind of fancy," she said. I asked her if she could identify him if she saw him again. "Definitely," she answered.

After calming her down a bit, I asked her to give me further details about the assault.

"I'm a nurse at the Veteran's Hospital on Lake Street, about three blocks from here," she said. "After I got off my late-night shift, I stopped for a quick drink at a bar."

"Which bar?" I asked. She told me.

"Did you notice anyone follow you from the bar?" I asked. She said she hadn't.

"What happened then?" I asked.

"As I entered the parking garage—*this* garage—I started getting out of my car," she said. "Suddenly—out of nowhere—this guy was right outside my car door, and he started messing with me—started trying to rape me. I yelled and tried to fight him off, but he was much too strong. He asked me where my condo was, and I told him. I thought he'd kill me otherwise. He took me in there and"—she began sobbing and her voice became thick again—"raped me over and over. For several hours, I think."

She told me the rapist finally left her, fleeing on foot—but not before leaving the victim bruised and badly shaken. She immediately called the police, and I had responded within minutes after her call.

I called the Inspectors' detail assigned to the possible-serial-rapes case. While waiting, I protected the crime scene and called for an ambulance to transport the victim to the emergency hospital for a check-up and rape exam. The Inspectors' unit arrived quickly, along with the crime lab unit. The crime scene was gone over thoroughly. This included a dusting of the victim's car for fingerprints.

We caught a break. A partial palm print was lifted from the doorframe of the victim's car. She also subsequently identified the suspect in a photo line-up. He was among several African-American men the cops suspected of being involved in rapes in the area. A pick-up order was issued on the following Monday. The cops conducted a stake-out—which soon proved fruitful—and the suspect was apprehended that Monday afternoon by the Inspectors' unit. He then was brought to Richmond Station for interrogation, after which he was booked.

In the meantime, the suspect's car—a big Oldsmobile—had been driven down to Richmond Station after his apprehension, and was parked in front. The keys, along with an inventory receipt for the contents of the car, were held by the booking officer at the station for later transport to the police garage.

The next day, Tuesday afternoon, when I came on duty, I received a call from the Inspectors that there was mistake at the city prison and our suspect had been released. The Inspectors believed they didn't have sufficient evidence against him.

That soon turned around.

The Inspectors discovered the suspect had several "priors" for which he was wanted by the police, and also that he'd committed parole violations. We then learned he was on his way to the station to pick up his Oldsmobile. We were to greet him and place him under arrest again. We were itching to get this guy back in "the bucket" (jail).

Since his Oldsmobile was parked in front of the station—and he might have another set of keys and simply be able to drive off—I needed to get him to come into the station without alerting him. So I went out to his car and took off the distributor cap, disabling the vehicle.

About an hour passed and in comes the suspect. True to our rape victim's account, he was a fancy-dressing, good-looking black man. I went up to him and asked, "Can I help you?"

"Yeah," he said. "I'm here to pick up my car, but it won't start. I might need a tow."

We went back out to his Oldsmobile, and he tried it again. The engine groaned and whined, but, of course, wouldn't start. I successfully hid my smirk.

At that time, I said to him, "Okay, then. You can use our phone to call out. Come back into the office."

As soon as he was within our office, before he knew what happened, I placed him under arrest and cuffed him. He was transported back to the city prison.

A few months later, the rapist's trial was held at the Hall of Justice. I was called to testify as to my role in the case. As it turned out, the suspect was charged with several assaults on women. In fact, he had a long history of such offenses, and had served time in state prison for them.

The suspect was found guilty as charged. Because of his long list of prior rapes, he was sentenced to life in prison. He would never set foot in the outside world again.

406: Officer Needs Assistance

The day of the sentencing, as I was leaving the courtroom, I passed right by the rapist. As I did, he reached out, fiercely grabbed my left wrist, looked at me with lifeless eyes, and said in a very sinister voice, "I'll kill you for this."

And I believed him.

Wealth Does Not a Gentleman Make

The patrol area assigned to the Richmond Station included some of the wealthiest sections of San Francisco. One of the most historic and publicized of those areas is Pacific Heights.

One night during my rookie year, while working the midnight to 10 a.m. watch in the Richmond 4 car, the stillness at 3:30 a.m. suddenly was interrupted:

"All cars . . . any Richmond car . . . Richmond 4 . . . a report of a possible 419 (fight, weapons involved) . . . the 400 block of Presidio Avenue . . . Code 3 (red light and siren)."

"10-4," I acknowledged. "Richmond 4 . . . 10-4."

A couple of minutes later, I rolled up to the 400 block of Presidio Avenue. About mid-block—in front of a big, luxurious apartment building—I was flagged down by a middle-aged woman dressed in a sheer nightgown, spotted all over with what later was determined to be her own blood.

At the same moment, John Wydler in the Richmond 1 car rolled onto the scene as my back-up. We jumped out of our respective radio cars and ran to the distraught woman. As we approached her, we could see trauma to her face, and that she was bleeding from her mouth and nose.

John went to his car and radioed for an ambulance. By this time—and despite the late-night hour—a few neighbors had gathered around the scene.

"He did it again!" I heard one bystander say.

"One of these days, he'll kill her," another one said.

We took the victim aside and asked her what happened. "My husband worked me over," she said through her tears. "He came home drunk . . . and . . . and . . . he kept drinking after he got home. I . . . tried to get him to stop. But he hit me after I spoke to him. He hit me and knocked me down." She managed to call the

49

police, and then ran out of the house onto the street, which is where we found her.

While we were talking with her and attempting to comfort her until the ambulance arrived, her husband made his appearance. He was a grotesquely fat man wearing a silk smoking jacket, swaying back and forth and pointing his finger at us.

"What the fuck are you jerks doing with my wife?" he yelled at us contemptuously. He lunged at her, and I had to separate the two of them. After that, I put her in the back of the squad car to keep her safe.

The fat man was obviously drunk as hell, and, if nothing else, this allowed us to place him under arrest. This was in 1959—prior to the Miranda ruling—so we didn't have to read him his rights. He was going to jail, plain and simple. We called for the paddy wagon to chauffeur him.

During the next twenty minutes, as we waited for the wagon, the handcuffed suspect continued to drunkenly harangue us.

"You won't get away with this!" he snarled. "I'll have your jobs over this! I'll put your asses in jail for false arrest! You don't know who you're messing with—but you'll soon find out!"

The paddy wagon finally arrived, and transported the suspect to Richmond Station. He was booked on public drunkenness charges (for starters).

In the meantime, John and I followed the victim to Park Emergency Hospital to interview her. As we waited outside her room, the ER doctor strode up to us, a serious expression on his face.

"I know you are the police officers working the case," he said, "so let me tell you what's happening. Luckily, none of her injuries are as serious as we first feared. She has some loose teeth, a broken nose, and some scrapes."

We thanked him for the update and he quickly walked away.

By the time we interviewed the victim, she had begun to calm down. She started relating her story again, in greater detail.

"My husband came home drunk . . . he was in a fighting mood. I guess I made it clear I didn't like it, because then he started punching me around."

She told us this was not the first time.

"I grabbed a kitchen knife to try to defend myself. But—luckily . . . *thank God!*—no one was injured by it. I left it in the kitchen when I ran out into the street."

Then she looked up at us and said, very seriously, "This is it. This is the last straw. I can't keep living like this. I want to press charges."

We called Richmond Station and advised the booking officer we were adding battery (felony assault) charges to the husband's public-drunkenness charge.

It wasn't until later that morning that we learned the victim and suspect were actually members of San Francisco's elite social set. The suspect was the owner and founder of a major Bay Area real-estate development company, and was very prominent in city government.

The case went to court, and a deal soon was cut. The husband was found guilty of public drunkenness and given probation.

Several months later, the headlines of the *San Francisco Chronicle* and *Examiner* newspapers lit up about the couple's impending divorce and the multi-millions of dollars at stake.

There is an interesting post-script to this story, one of hope and affirmation for battered women:

Eventually—after she left her abusive husband—the victim developed her own cookware business and became extremely successful. She even had her own, very popular cooking show on local San Francisco television.

The suspect moved from the Presidio Avenue address, and continued to be a jerk.

Fortunately, I had no further contact with the man, nor did he make good on his threat to "have my job."

I learned an important message from this episode:

Wealth and social standing do not a gentleman make. Nor do they make one immune to spousal abuse.

"The Beatnik Cop" and "Big Daddy" Nord

As beatnik culture began coming into San Francisco in the 1950s, tension started rising between many "average citizens" and police officers like me. This was the first counter-culture wave, which would eventually culminate in the drug activity and sometimes-lawlessness of the hippies and various politically radical groups, such as the Black Panthers. Suddenly we, as cops, were dealing with a lot more people who seemed to embody a "couldn't care less" attitude, who'd sleep outdoors in the park if they felt like it—that kind of thing. A lot of middle-class homeowners and families felt threatened by the new atmosphere enveloping the city. The marijuana . . . the odd dress . . . the "anti-establishment" attitude . . . the seemingly random destruction of property . . . all these things were first brought into San Francisco by the beatniks. And they quickly caused a cultural divide.

To a cop like me, these people seemed to assume the attitude of *I'm going to cause trouble.* A lot of times this was political in nature, and the so-called captains of the beatnik movement could see they were gathering support among many average San Franciscans. People like Eric "Big Daddy" Nord (see below) and Timothy Leary started to gain rabid followings.

To try to counter the lawlessness of some of the beatniks, a cop named Bill Bigarani was asked to go underground and infiltrate the "movement." The San Francisco Police Officers Association was getting heat from the media and public for the heightened crime and drug use around the city, so Bigarani's mission was deemed especially critical.

Bigarani's undercover operation took him to the heart of the San Francisco beatnik "scene," which had been popularized in such best-selling novels as Jack Kerouac's *On the Road*. Bigarani dressed like a beatnik, hung out with members of that community, then reported back to the Police Department regarding his investigations. Because the beatniks were the first-ever group in San Francisco to engage in widespread marijuana, heroin, and other drug use, their presence spurred a wave of drug-related burglaries, larcenies, muggings, assaults, and murders. "The Beatnik Cop" investigated all of this while underground. He even wrote training manuals for us cops, regarding the best ways to make beatnik-related drug busts or de-escalate situations that otherwise might explode into violence.

Ultimately, Bigarani's efforts resulted in regular—sometimes weekly—raids on drug and other criminal hide-outs. Bigarani eventually was promoted to captain.

Not long after—because of his popularity with the cops and citizens who knew about his work as "The Beatnik Cop"—Bigarani began to have political aspirations. His supporters urged him to run for sheriff on a reform platform. He took the plunge, and, in the October 1971 edition of *The San Francisco Police Officers' Association Notebook* (newspaper) he wrote an open letter that read, in part:

My Brother Officers:

As you well know, I have been endorsed in my candidacy for Sheriff by the Executive Board of our Association, and subsequently endorsed unanimously at our last general membership meeting . . . .

I have done extensive research on the Sheriff's Department over the past two years, and have come to the conclusion which, in my opinion should be obvious to all, [that] the present administration is laboring under a major misapprehension of the seriousness of the problems involved, and is sorely lacking in leadership and management.

"The Beatnik Cop" went on to declare in the open letter "that a reorganization of the entire department is necessary" and that he had "the programs to cure these ills and provide the citizen-taxpayer with the essential services to which he is entitled."

But it wasn't to be. Bigarani's clean-up-the-sheriff's-department campaign was doomed almost from the start. The moneyed-interests in the city stepped in and opposed him, and his campaign never got any real traction. That's a shame, because Bill Bigarani was a serious-minded person and he could have done a lot of good.

* * *

Another real "character" from those beatnik days was Eric Nord, whom newspaper columnists called "the king of the Beat Generation." Known to his friends and the media as "Big Daddy," Nord was a 6-foot, 8-inch bear of a man who, toward the end of his life, weighed more than 400 pounds. His greatest claim to fame was as owner of the beatnik nightclub called the *hungry i*, where famous performers such as Bill Cosby, Mort Sahl, and the Kingston Trio got their start. (Regarding the name of his club, Nord once told interviewers, "I was going to call it the Hungry Intellectual, but I ran out of paint for the sign.")

Nord and the *hungry i* were later credited—by the *Los Angeles Times* and others—with helping to establish the "beat movement" in California. Born in Germany and about as eccentric as they come, Nord was known to prowl San Francisco's North Beach using a giant tricycle for transportation.

Nord may have seemed like a harmless flake, but—for cops like me—he spelled trouble. He was certainly no friend of the establishment or of the police department. He was a pain in the neck. He was very vocal—obviously a smart guy—and young people were attracted to his natural leadership ability. He formed a faction with young, rebellious people, and helped encourage youthful rebellion.

In June 1958—in an attempt to crack down on drug use and delinquency in North Beach—San Francisco mayor George Christopher ordered a raid of one of Nord's clubs. "Big Daddy" was arrested for operating a public dance without a license. The raid resulted in a public spat with the cops that Nord seemed to enjoy.

After a while, the word got out that we cops should leave Nord alone as much as legally possible. Otherwise, we'd just be helping to fan the flames of his rebellion.

Eventually Nord and the beatniks were eclipsed by the hippies and the "flower power" generation. Little was heard from him after the 1960s. But I still clearly recall the tumultuous times in San Francisco that "Big Daddy" embodied.

CENTRAL STATION STORIES

Central Station

My second assignment was at Central Station, located on Kearny Street between Clay and Washington Streets.

The old Hall of Justice was also on Kearny – between Clay and California Streets – a block from our station. The Hall of Justice was there until the mid '60's when it moved to a new building at 850 Bryant at 7th Street.

This was an extremely diverse area in all ways................Chinese and Italians lived in most of the apartments, flats and homes...and owned a large part of the restaurants, bars, clothing stores, hardware stores, etc. But, the French Church and school– Notre Dame des Victoires – were in the middle of this district. The large San Francisco French community came from all over the city to attend this church and school at the edge of Chinatown and the financial district.

Tadich's, Paoli's, The Leopard, the Blue Fox, Original Joes, the Gold Spike, The Green Mill, Caesars, San Remo, North Beach Restaurant, LaRocca's Corner – these are merely a small sampling of the many restaurants and bars serving the locals and the many tourists.

Chinatown was packed with people at all times......locals as well as tourists. Most Chinese lived in small rooms, many family members to a room, with little space between one apartment and another.

They had a Chinese Catholic School for their children to attend...as well as many public schools.

In the North Beach area – the entertainment venues included the notorious Condor Club where Carol Doda – before and after – performed her topless show. She didn't always have that huge chest! The Playboy Club – run by a Novato neighbor of ours - , the Hungry I, Purple Onion, Facks, were also there. Bimbo's was a huge club, with the "girl in the fishbowl" appearing nightly. Finocchio's was famous for its drag queen shows. Gold Street had "girls on swings and trapezes and in bird cages". Tourists enjoyed this nightlife.....

Many stars got their start in these clubs........Barbra Streisand, Phyllis Diller, many folk singing groups, and comedians Mort Sahl, Shecky Greene, Lenny Bruce – among others.

Fugazi Hall, Cafferata Ravioli Factory, Fior d'Italia – plus the Big Hotels....The Fairmont, Mark Hopkins, Stanford Ct., Huntington....and on and on.

Sts Peter and Paul Church was the mainstay of the large Italian Catholic community, and Washington Square was a welcome oasis of greenery among the steep hills – some with stairs to help the climb.

This area was noted for its good weather, too. Not too much fog, more moderate temps, sunny most days. Of course, if the entire city was rainy or foggy, so were these neighborhoods. The good weather facilitated the busy nightlife.......usually bustling with out-of-towners.

A lot of changes have occurred in this area of SF - old-time restaurants have closed, the old entertainment houses have shut down or changed their type of venue, some "cleaning up" of Chinatown and surrounding streets. The Central Distric was popular with tourists. But it was a very tough piece of real estate.

Up Close and Personal

Several months into my rookie year, I was transferred from the Richmond Station to the Central Station. The Central district included the heart of the city, from Nob Hill to the Tenderloin. At this time—the late 1950s—the Tenderloin was known for its strip clubs, gay bars, restaurants, and "watering holes."

Most of the district's strip bars were located on the infamous Mason Street. One of the more notable ones was called The Horse and Cow. It was owned by George Looby, a great friend and supporter of the police department. George, it was known, had helped undercover cops with their investigations, and, on more than one occasion, had helped inspectors and beat cops nab suspected criminals by "keeping his eyes peeled." Even though The Horse and Cow was a strip bar, it was a clean, respectable joint. (Or as "respectable" as a strip bar can be.)

One 4 p.m. to 12 a.m. watch, I was assigned a walking beat with veteran officer "Red" McCibben. Our beat area included Mason Street.

At this time, I was twenty-one years old—barely old enough to legally go into these establishments. And I did not have a great deal of experience with strip bars or—to say the least—with strippers. I think Red guessed this when he saw my eyes pop out of my head as we passed before The Horse and Cow, with its posters out front of the featured dancers. Initially we simply walked past the establishment, but, after a few seconds, Red said, "We'll go in there later for coffee."

Around 10 p.m. that night things were pretty quiet, so Red turned to me and said, "Ya ready for some coffee, Ray? Let's go grab some at The Horse and Cow. I'll introduce you to George Looby."

We made our way over to the establishment, through the heavy, red velvet drapes that separated the sidewalk traffic from the bar and stage. The interior was dimly lit, with most of the light reflecting from a small, elevated stage. As we walked in, the stage was occupied by a scantily clad woman doing her interpretation of some type of dance. The audience included about twelve men, mostly young, including several sailors on leave. (The Horse and Cow was one of the few San Francisco bars not off-limits to the military. George Looby was a retired seaman, and his place was well known to military men.)

Red brought me over to the end of the bar, toward a big man about fifty years old and as bald as Mr. Clean. It was George Looby.

"George, this is Officer Ray Petersen," Red said. "Ray's the new kid on the block. The new cop kid."

"Great . . . welcome, Ray," George said. "Here . . . let me pour you a cup of coffee." He proceeded to pour me a cup of java that tasted like it was three days old.

"This coffee reminds me of my days at sea," George said.

"Yeah, once you've drunk this, you'd never forget the experience," I replied, which luckily drew smiles from George and Red.

After a lot of small talk, George turned to me and said, "Hey, Ray, you ever heard of Baby Doll? She's my featured dancer."

"Um . . . can't say . . . uh . . . that I have," I stammered back, trying to hide the bright red hue spreading across my face.

George grinned and waved toward the shadows around the stage area. Moments later, a dark, difficult-to-see figure started moving toward us. Suddenly, thanks to the lights bouncing off the back bar, I caught sight of this beautiful creature. In a moment she was standing right in front of us, wearing nothing but a G-string, pasties, and a warm smile. One could say we were "up close and personal." As we all stood there, I could feel my face getting even hotter and turning from beet-red to beet-redder. When they observed my predicament, Red, George, and Baby Doll mercilessly began to tease me (no pun intended). George got a huge kick out of seeing how red my face had gotten.

As it turned out, Baby Doll was a twenty-five year old student at San Francisco State College, engaged to a San Francisco police officer. None of that mattered, however, as I tried to avoid gluing my eyes to her ample assets.

What a way to be introduced to the world of dance.

Compassion

I'm sure Sgt. Al Rosenbaum would not have considered himself a teacher or role model, but I thought he was. Sgt. Rosenbaum was a gruff, thirty-year veteran of the San Francisco Police Department, whose brother was a noted columnist for the *San Francisco Chronicle*. Most of Sgt. Rosenbaum's thirty years on the force had been spent as a booking sergeant at the city prison. According to Sgt. Rosenbaum, it was his choice of assignments.

As a rookie and probation officer, I was sent on various details when and as needed. One such detail was weekend relief at the city prison. I worked this detail several times during my first year of duty. On many occasions I was assigned to Sgt. Rosenbaum's watch. After a period of time, I learned to appreciate this as a unique opportunity to grow as a police officer and as a man.

The city prison held inmates serving sentences of up to one year. It also was used after the daily arrests of suspects awaiting arraignment on anything from common drunkenness to murder. The traffic in and out of the city prison was quite hectic. In addition to the multiple transfers of prisoners from district stations, there was an endless stream of attorneys, clergy, medical staff, prisoner's family members, and other police officers. You saw a cross-section of humanity without benefit of make-up. It often was quite ugly. (It was particularly ugly the night I saw an old high school acquaintance in the paddy wagon. He was being arrested for a very serious criminal act.)

As a watch commander, Sgt. Rosenbaum ran a tight ship. He let you know, up front, that he didn't care much for the new kids on the block. Or for many of the old-timers, either. He built a shield around himself—usually projecting a tremendously sarcastic attitude—which I believe was his way of avoiding being vulnerable. That's how he survived such a tough assignment all those years.

One thing Sgt. Rosenbaum refused to tolerate was a physically or verbally abusive police officer. His attitude was, "An officer has the right to defend himself, but no more." He was especially watchful of the treatment of drunks—repeat-offenders in particular. The streets of San Francisco were full of souls addicted to alcohol, who eventually wound up in the city prison. When asked about them, Sgt. Rosenbaum would always emphatically say, "These people are human beings. They are someone's son, daughter, husband, father, or mother. And they deserve to be treated with respect."

Whenever he saw a cop treating an inmate disrespectfully—or unnecessarily pushing them or verbally abusing them—he'd go ballistic.

"You don't have any idea what life brings to some people," he'd snarl at the officer. "I will not have you treating people badly on my watch."

Sgt. Rosenbaum's deep-seated compassion affected me and served me well. Many times, while on the police force, I would remind myself of his remarks while dealing with some nasty, disgusting human being. His compassion helped me develop a tolerance and personal strength I might not have otherwise had.

I See You There

Frank Kalafate and I were working Operation S in plainclothes and in an unmarked radio car. Frank was a quiet, good-hearted guy. He complemented me well, and I was always fond of him. We were sharing an idle conversation when suddenly, at around 1:30 a.m., an all-channel call came through:

"Hot prowl (event happening *now*) at the Broadway Manor Motel . . . Broadway and Van Ness . . . suspect seen leaving the unit through the second-story sliding glass door."

We were about two blocks away so we acknowledged, "10-4 .. . S-4 responding," and rolled in.

Several police cars responded at the same time, mostly uniformed officers from Central and Northern stations. I never liked "hot" crime scenes hit all at once by lots of cops. They could be dangerous as hell, because you often couldn't tell the good guys from the bad guys. And being in plainclothes might make us appear to be possible suspects to the uniformed officers.

Upon arrival on the scene, Frank and I elected to park on Van Ness, north of Broadway. Next to the motel on that block, there were many multi-unit private residences. I left the car and started running toward the crime scene.

"There!" I yelled to Frank behind me. I pointed and ran into an alley behind the building adjacent to the motel. In the dim, spotty light back there, I could see a fence, a shadow-laced yard, and the motel parking lot, which separated me from the second story of the motel.

I waved my flashlight across the area and, much to my surprise, almost instantly caught the suspect in my beam.

This is crazy, I thought. *What are the chances?*

"Freeze!" I yelled. "Put your hands in the air or you're a dead man!"

I saw him hesitate, look around, and then put up his hands. He did have a gun.

I was lucky as hell, because he didn't realize there was no way I could get to him from where I was standing. I was on the other side of the fence. But my sudden appearance and commanding voice froze him—at least long enough for two uniformed officers to reach him and place him under arrest.

And there was another thing the suspect, luckily, didn't know:

The gun I was training on him was a two-inch .38 special that couldn't hit the broad side of a barn. I would have better luck *throwing* the gun at him.

But his ignorance was my bliss.

And our apprehension of the suspect temporarily helped reduce crime statistics in that "motel row" part of San Francisco. After we arrested and booked the suspect, he was quickly linked to several other unsolved break-ins in the area.

You Never Know What You're Going to See

One night I was working the 12 a.m. to 8 a.m. watch out of Central Station. I was assigned a particular walking beat that included the Financial District east of Montgomery Street.

Probably needless to say, there wasn't a great deal of visible activity that night, especially as the clock ticked toward 3 a.m. The thousands of people who worked in the Financial District had long since gone home for the night. Therefore, when I saw the cream-colored sedan parked in the far corner of an empty self-parking lot, I was curious.

From where I was standing, it appeared there was someone in the car. Every once in awhile, I thought I saw a head pop up. During this time, there had been an increasing number of office break-ins in the area, so I knew I had to check this out.

I headed toward the car with my gun at the ready (holster unsnapped), with my flashlight in hand. As I drew closer to the car, I called out, "Police officer!" and shined my flashlight into the car.

I'll never forget what I saw next.

As I waved my flashlight around the car, its beam suddenly fell on two very bare behinds. Seconds later, an arm shot up and my light caught a badge in the hand of one of San Francisco's finest.

No doubt what I'd happened upon was . . . um . . . an intimate interrogation.

I immediately walked away, and never did find out who was in the car. But I'm sure that—at least for a while—I stopped that interrogation cold.

I Don't Know Where
It Came From

During one midnight-to-8 a.m. watch, I was working the 2 car out of Central Station. My partner at the time was a good ol' boy everyone called "Houston," because he was originally from Texas. Houston was about thirty-two, thus a lot older than me. His Texas drawl made him a fish-out-of-water in San Francisco, but he was a nice guy and didn't seem to mind the good-natured ribbing he sometimes took.

At about 3 a.m.—the bewitching hour—the dispatcher suddenly lit up our radio, and seconds later we were responding to a robbery call at the Stewart Hotel on Powell Street.

Upon arrival at the front of the hotel, we were greeted by a man and woman in the midst of a heated argument. The man—tastefully attired in boxer shorts, shoes with no socks, a T-shirt, and a sport coat—immediately started bellowing at us as we arrived.

"Arrest this woman!" he yelled, pointing at the attractive, middle-aged woman standing next to him.

Dressed in high heels, a cocktail dress, and a fur coat, the woman calmly looked at us and said, "Arrest me? I've done nothing wrong. This guy is just drunk, that's all."

This was rapidly shaping up to be a muddy "he said, she said" situation, so Houston and I immediately separated the two complainants to get their separate stories, trying to get some clarity on what had happened. Houston took the man—the alleged victim—back up to the man's hotel room, and I took the woman and put her in the back seat of the patrol car.

The man proceeded to tell Houston the following story:

"I met her at Tiny's," he said. Tiny's was a well-known breakfast place on Powell Street. "We went up to my room to get . .

. you know . . . better acquainted." After what was no doubt a long conversation, the man fell asleep, he said.

"When I woke up, the broad was gone, and so was $1,000 of my hard-earned cash. That's when I called you guys—the cops."

Meanwhile—and probably needless to say—the woman in my patrol car was loudly protesting her innocence, saying she couldn't believe she was in the back of a cop car, after doing nothing wrong.

"If I were guilty of anything, do you honestly think I would have stuck around till you cops showed up?" she asked.

A good point, I had to admit. After leaving the man's room, the woman *had* stayed in the hotel lobby, until the man came downstairs, relocated her, and brought her outside to face the cops.

Before I'd put the woman in the back of our patrol car, I had—for her safety as well as mine—handcuffed her hands behind her back. During the course of our conversation, she confirmed to me she wasn't exactly a Girl Scout.

"Okay, yeah, I'm a working girl," she admitted, after some intense interrogation on my part. "And yeah, that guy is one of my johns. But I didn't take any money from him, other than my hourly rate."

Events soon proved otherwise.

While we were talking, I noticed the woman fumbling around behind her back, even though she was cuffed.

What the heck is she doing? I wondered.

I was curious, so I reached over the seat and pushed her aside. As she moved and bent forward, I immediately spied some currency, all bundled and crumpled up behind her. I grabbed the money—nearly $1,000—as the woman laughably claimed she had "no idea where that money came from."

Right, I thought. *And I have no idea why you think I'd believe that.*

In the meantime, Houston had completed his interrogation of the alleged victim, and they returned from his hotel room.

While with Houston, the man had coughed up more details about the incident:

"I'm from out of town," he'd told Houston. (He also admitted he was married.) "I was out drinking—pretty heavily, I guess—and I eventually wandered into Tiny's for a late-night snack. When I went to pay my bill, I must have flashed my thick wallet, because, before I knew it, this attractive woman—the one you saw me with—moved from her seat by the cashier over next to me. At first I was clueless as to what she was. But then, after a while, it sunk in. So I asked if she'd like to . . . well, you know . . . and we struck a deal.

"But there was something suspicious about her, so when we got back to my room I hid $1,000 in my shoe. She must have seen me do that, though, because when I dozed off, she made her move."

Once the woman was confronted, she finally admitted the theft. She even told me, "I always check their shoes, because they always seem to put their money there." She was officially placed under arrest, and the paddy wagon was called to transfer her to the city prison. The victim went back to his room—embarrassed and lighter in his wallet—wondering how he was going to explain to his wife his visit to San Francisco's nightlife.

A Little Levity

It was about 2:30 a.m. and Mark and I were in our sector, patrolling the Financial District. Mark was an athletically-built guy with a short temper. He was an excellent cop who was very interested in one day making inspector (detective). During the six months that I worked with him, he was single but seriously dating a young nurse at one of the emergency hospitals.

On this particular night, it started to become very windy outside, and we both knew what that meant: Soon there would be a rash of alarms going off as the large glass doors on city buildings began to rattle with the wind. The Financial district always seemed to be especially windy.

Whenever an alarm went off like that, there was a particular protocol that was followed:

First, the alarm company—and, soon after, us cops—would be dispatched to the premises. Their rep generally would have a key to the building, so he would let us all in. Upon entering, we would search to determine if there was any reason—aside from wind or some other benevolent force—for the triggering of the alarm.

Over a period of time, we grew to learn the specific locations of alarms that repeatedly would go off due to nothing more than strong winds. The situation was getting so out-of-hand that the San Francisco police department was seriously discussing cutting off response to those buildings until the problem was solved. Bogus alarms took a lot of cop time and attention away from serious situations.

There was another standard element in these situations, too. Most of the alarm companies would hire what we used to call "rent-a-cop" types to inspect buildings after alarms had gone off. (The rent-a-cops generally were not allowed to carry a weapon.) After awhile, we got to know several of these guys and their MO fairly well. Usually they were eager to please, and wanted to do the search. When the building involved was a large, multi-level store, their eagerness was welcome.

On this particular night when the alarm went off, it was the third time that night at that same store. The alarm rep was a college student, studying to be a cop. To say he was eager would be the understatement of the year.

Inside the entrance of the store, there was a display that included a male mannequin standing with his hand extended. The store was pitch-black except for the street lights and our flashlights. Suddenly—I'm not sure why—a mischievous impulse seized me, and I whispered to Mark, "Let's have some fun." Mark had an expression on his face that said, *What the heck are you talking about?*

He soon would find out.

While our eager young man was doing his thing, I went over to the mannequin and took its hand off. I then placed the hand up my sleeve, trying hard to hide my smirk.

When the search was over, I went over to the young rent-a-cop and extended my hand—or, the *mannequin's* hand—to shake hands and thank him for his good work. As he grabbed my fake hand, I said, "Thanks," and just walked away, leaving the fake hand shaking his. A moment later *"Aaahhhhhhhhhhhhhhhhhh !!!!"* was reverberating around the building, as the eager young rent-a-cop threw his hands up in the air and began screaming. The look on his face was priceless. Even Mark thought so.

Later, I felt bad about this incident, so I sought out the rent-a-cop.

"I'm sorry," I said. "I shouldn't have done that to you."

By then he had calmed down, and his response was quite unexpected.

"Aw, don't worry about it, Ray," he said. "I actually think it was very funny."

But I noticed he didn't shake my hand.

After Hours Tour

In the early 1960's, San Francisco saw an increase in so-called "after hours clubs." Most of them were located in the section of the city known as the Tenderloin, an area not far from Union Square in central San Francisco. The Clift, the St. Francis and the Sir Francis Drake were prominent hotels in the area. As a police officer who frequently was on patrol in the area, I'd see people like Willie Mays and other celebrities walking around down there. But that didn't mean it wasn't a high-crime area. It certainly was. And after hours clubs—and the "element" they attracted—were a major contributor.

After hours clubs were frequented by curious tourists and creatures from the underworld. A major percentage of crimes committed in the Tenderloin—and perhaps beyond the Tenderloin—were committed by club attendees.

A typical after-hours club would be located either above daytime businesses or below street level. They usually were very dark and illuminated by neon signs. Most clubs had some type of live music. The waitresses worked mostly for tips. The reason the term "after hours club" was coined was that these clubs were open between 2 a.m. and 6 a.m., when liquor could not legally be sold in San Francisco. Note the word "legally," because liquor, in fact, was widely sold in these clubs during those hours.

That's where the San Francisco police department had to step in.

Law enforcement could see the situation was getting out of control, and something had to be done. So two major strategies were developed—the use of undercover cops and the use of an "After Hours Detail."

First, undercover cops assigned to the Vice Detail gathered information used to try to close these establishments. These officers would pose as ordinary customers and try to make an illegal purchase of alcohol and/or arrange a prostitution deal. If the cop was successful and evidence was developed, it would be forwarded to the Licensing Bureau. Soon thereafter, the legal process would be initiated, by which the violator's business would be closed down. For a business owner, this was typically much worse than being arrested.

The other effective way we cops "leaned on" after hours clubs was through good old-fashioned harassment involving an "After Hours Detail."

Here's how it worked:

The first step was to have a sergeant and three or four patrolmen designated as the After Hours Detail. The detail would then meet at a pre-determined street corner, and proceed to make their rounds. During the 2 a.m. to 6 a.m. after hours club time frame, each cop would go into each known club several times. They would engage the patrons in dialogue meant to be uncomfortable or even, in some cases, embarrassing.

After each such conversation, a 3" by 5" Field Interrogation Card would be completed by the officer. The card was kept on file and later reviewed, especially if some type of crime had just been committed in the area. Many times a good witness—or even a suspect—was uncovered via the Field Interrogation Card. This type of continual police engagement hurt the businesses and, in many cases, eventually shut them down.

What's in the Bag?

Harry Paretchan and I were working the Central 3 car during the 4 p.m. to midnight watch. Harry was an outgoing, efficient, personable, well-liked guy. He was also very political. (He later became a fireman and served as officer of the fireman's union.) I liked Harry and enjoyed working with him.

Our patrol area that night included Chinatown, with all its mystique and cultural differences. The Chinatown in San Francisco was one of the largest in any U.S. city. It had a strange atmosphere, with citizens who were deeply suspicious of the police. You got the sense that there was a real underground world there—a lot of underground gambling and drug-dealing. The cops used to say, "If you want to lose somebody, take him to Chinatown."

Another thing we understood about Chinatown was its citizens' typical refusal to engage with the police. It was rare for a request for police assistance to come from there. You could have a body on the floor with forty-seven bullet holes in it, but they still wouldn't ask the cops for help. The Asian culture taught its citizens to handle their own problems, with no outside help. So with this in mind, Harry and I genuinely were intrigued when we were dispatched to the Chinatown YMCA hotel to deal with a "418" (fight in progress).

As we arrived at the YMCA, we were greeted by the Chinese manager, flailing his arms around and yelling loudly and excitedly at us. There was one problem, however: We couldn't understand a single word he said. After we calmed him down, the manager pointed excitedly upward with one finger and said, in very broken English, "Big fight! Big fight!" Third floor!"

Harry and I gestured for him to follow us up there, to show us the exact room. As we ascended the staircase, the manager kept yelling, "I want dem out! I want all dem out!"

Then, as we reached the third floor, all hell broke loose.

Suddenly two bodies came crashing through a door, landing at our feet in the hallway. Seconds later, three more bodies followed. In a flash, we took in the scene—five males at our feet, all dressed in some type of olive-green military uniform. It was apparent these men had been drinking heavily, which helped fuel the situation.

Shaking his head in disgust, the Chinese manager turned to us and said in his heavily accented English, "Dese men army officers. From Thailand. Dey been here two day. Nothing but trouble. Nothing but trouble, dey are. Want them out!"

But that was easier said than done.

As we soon learned, we'd been invited into a complex international situation. The U.S. government and Thailand had a military arrangement to house the men while they were being processed, prior to their departure back to Thailand. It seems the U.S. was training officers from Thailand on a regular basis, and Fort Baker in San Francisco was the port of debarkation as these men left the U.S. (This was during the time when U.S. involvement in the Vietnam War was escalating. The U.S. government was thus training some of the forces of its ally, Thailand, in the hopes of keeping that country free from communist invasion or coup.)

Once we received this background on the situation, Harry and I determined this was a Military Police issue—not a job for the San Francisco police force. But when I called the Military Police command post and explained the situation, the MP captain shot back, "We don't want to touch that. You guys need to handle it as you see fit."

That, of course, put us in complete limbo. So after I hung up the phone, I said to Harry, "Let's get these guys packed up and out of here. Where they go after that isn't our problem."

Going into their room, we began to gather their belongings together. But as I picked up a duffel bag, one of the Thai soldiers suddenly ran across the room and jumped me from behind, hitting me over the head with *his* duffel bag. The other four joined in, but Harry and I managed to get the situation quickly under control. We requested a paddy wagon and, once it arrived, the five suspects were transported to Central Station.

Harry and I stayed at the hotel to take inventory of the suspects' property. I picked up a duffel bag, noticing how unusually heavy it felt. I unzipped it and, there before me, were several handguns plus ammunition. All the weapons were still in the original packing material. The other bags in the room were pretty much the same. Within a matter of minutes, we'd discovered several dozen guns and several hundred rounds of ammunition.

What the hell's going on? we wondered.

It would eventually take us several hours to put the pieces of the puzzle together.

As we were pouring over the case, we again called the captain at the MP station. This time—very suddenly—he was extremely interested in our case. He contacted the FBI regarding the weapons we've discovered, and, the next thing we knew, Harry and I were knee-deep in an international incident. And numerous U.S. government agencies wanted in on the action.

The five Thai officers were transferred and then detained overnight by the MPs. The plan was that they were being shipped out of San Francisco at 8 a.m. the next morning. All the authorities stuck to that plan. The Thai soldiers were shipped home the next morning.

Later, Harry and I were told this incident lead to the uncovering of a major gun-smuggling operation, which apparently had been going on for some time. Waves of Thai soldiers had been coming into the U.S. for training, stealing big caches of weapons while they were here, then selling them back in Thailand for a pretty penny.

Almost inadvertently, Harry and I had put an end to that.

But there was an unsettling post-script to this story:

Our part in this incident took nearly twenty hours to wrap up. Harry and I didn't get off duty until around 6:30 a.m. When I got home, I went right to bed.

I wasn't in bed long.

Almost as soon as my head hit the pillow, my wife Priscilla woke me, telling me the captain from Central Station was on the phone. Priscilla handed me the receiver.

"Yes?" I said in a raspy, sleepy voice.

"Petersen, this is the deputy chief. We need to talk with you about the YMCA incident last night. I want you in my office within the hour."

After confirming I'd be there, I crawled out of bed and wearily put my clothes back on.

I arrived at Central Station within about forty-five minutes, and found a large crowd gathered in the front entrance. Everyone and his godfather was there—members of the media, U.S. military brass, and, of course, San Francisco police officers, including the Central Station captain. Word about the gun-smuggling bust had leaked.

When the deputy chief spotted me, he quickly came over.

"Ray," he said, "thanks for coming down. I know you and Harry had a long night. And I think we're all set now. You and Harry can go back home."

That was slightly annoying—given that I'd been awakened from a sound sleep to go there—but I kept my composure, understanding everyone was dealing with a very-out-of-the-ordinary situation.

"Why did you previously feel Harry and I had to come back here?" I asked.

"One of the Thai soldiers told us you and Harry had taken some of the guns. We had to check into that. We knew it was complete BS, but we had to check it out, anyway. Just doing our jobs."

The captain then explained to us the context of the accusation they'd just disproved:

When the FBI had contacted Fort Lewis, Washington regarding the stolen weapons, the serial numbers were checked. The FBI determined there were additional guns missing—beyond the ones Harry and I had rounded up—and, when asked about them, the Thais had lied and said Harry and I had taken them.

The accusation was immediately checked with U.S. government sources, and quickly proven to be unfounded. So that was that. We were free to go.

Harry continued to work the Chinatown detail for several years after that. He always felt that incident gave him a good idea of what to expect in that strange, mysterious sector of the city.

MISSION STATION STORIES

Mission Station

My third assignment, Mission Station, was located on Valencia Street between 23rd and 24th Streets, in the bowels of the inner Mission District.

This district was very large and eclectic, encompassing not only the flat, crowded Mission area, but also Diamond Heights. It also included the Castro, the Upper Market (or Duboce Triangle as it's now known), and the Eureka Valley and Noe Valley neighborhoods.

From the flatlands, where Mission Station was located, to the hills of Twin Peaks and Rocky Hill, you could view just about every landscape possible in one city. The hills of Noe Valley had many streets so steep you had to climbs stairs to get from one street to another.

Since we lived in the Duboce Triangle area, this assignment was easy for me in some ways. My in-laws, the Parodis, lived up the street and across the street from our flat, so a lot of nights my partners and I would enjoy Italian family meals with them.

Restaurants in the neighborhood reflected the many diverse ethnicities and nationalities of the population. The district had a majority (through steadily shrinking) Italian population, but many Mexican, Asian, and Irish families also lived there, with a smattering of Scandinavians.

Many Mom-'n-Pop-type restaurants were there, mostly in the inner Mission. These included Johnson's Mexican Tamale (yes, Johnson's!), Charlie's Tamales up on 18th Street in the Castro, Mel's Drive-In on South Van Ness, and our favorite, Bruno's Italian Place, which featured great food and live music. Bruno's was where many people would celebrate anniversaries, birthdays, and other special occasions. I think it's still there, in another incarnation.

Many other wonderful places dotted the Mission District landscape. There was Mission Dolores Basilica, where Priscilla and

I were married . . . the tiny old Mission next door to it . . . the huge Lucky Lager brewery . . . Joe's Club on 20th Street and York . . . Dolores Park and Duboce Park . . . Mission High School . . . Notre Dame High School . . . the Greek Orthodox Cathedral of the Annunciation, a huge new church for the Bay Area's very large Greek community . . . plus several other high schools, junior high schools, and grade schools. Most of the homes in the area were multi-family dwellings teeming with life.

Mission Street itself was a busy, bustling, polyglot area— anything you needed in San Francisco you likely could find there. Even at that time, the Hispanic population was huge, and it was common to hear people speaking Spanish and English in the same store. In fact, some *only* spoke Spanish.

The weather in the Mission District was nearly always perfect—mostly warm and sunny with very little fog or wind, especially in the flatlands of the inner Mission.

Some of the neighborhoods have gone through major changes since I worked there. But in my memory the District remains timeless.

Punk

Tim Thorsen and I were just arriving on duty at the Mission Station. This was for the 4 p.m. to midnight watch, and our watch commander was reading the orders of the day.

Normally this was a routine procedure. We'd hear a standard recap of the past day's crimes, particularly those committed in the Mission District. But this particular day we received something else—a special alert.

Since the Mission District was populated by residents and businesses of great ethnic variety, there was constant tension in the air. This was especially true within the younger generation, where there was an increasing amount of gang activity. This particular day, our lieutenant told us of a rumor that the cops had picked up—that there might be a gang fight at one of the local parks. Several gangs and weapons were to be involved. The only thing these gangs had in common was their hatred of the "pigs" (us cops).

After patrolling our sector for a couple of hours, Tim and I parked at Mel's Drive-In to have a cup of coffee and shoot the breeze with Jenny the carhop. Jenny was dating a cop from Southern Station. Mel's was a "safe" spot where our radio car crews could hang out and never be out of touch with communications. Besides, it was fun flirting with the carhops.

Suddenly, we were yanked back to reality. The dashboard radio lit up with an urgent call: "All cars . . . any Mission cars . . . 18th and Guerrero, Dolores Park . . . report of a 418 (gang fight with weapons involved)." The dispatcher told us of eye witnesses reporting beatings and other acts of violence, and that we needed to be very careful as we approached the scene.

"Mission 4, 10-4," we shot back, quickly putting away our coffee and saying a quick "See ya" to Jenny.

Since we were only ten blocks away, we were the first black-and-white to arrive on the scene. We came in like gangbusters—siren wailing and red light flashing.

The first thing we saw was a large crowd of young people, mostly males, starting to disperse as they heard us approach. That is, *most* of them dispersed. A few of the hard-core leaders refused to leave, and actually sat down in a circle around one of the well-known neighborhood tough guys, Chuck Wright. Chuck was nonchalantly lying on his side, as if he were sunning himself. Or maybe posing like a Roman emperor.

Tim and I had had prior run-ins with Chuck. For a seventeen-year old, he had an impressive track record—of the criminal variety. As the saying goes, "The chips don't fall far from the block," and that was certainly true of Chuck. His father was a graduate of San Quentin, and his older brother was doing undergraduate time there.

As we approached Chuck and his tough-guy buddies, Tim and I were shouting to the crowd to continue to disperse. But Chuck lay there defiantly, putting on his best thug face and spitting back at us, "This park is open to the public, pigs! I ain't going anywhere."

"You're wrong about that," I snarled back, bending over the young thug, grabbing him by his arm, pulling him to his feet, and putting him in a head-lock. As I was doing so, a switchblade fell from Chuck's pocket. Switchblades were illegal.

"That ain't mine," he grunted.

"Yeah, right," I said as I placed him under arrest, which he responded to with a torrent of "fuck you's!"

Chuck's buddies started to regroup and the air crackled with a tense, dangerous vibe. Chuck began to struggle as I walked him to the radio car, and the next second he was screaming, "Kill the pig shit!" and several other epithets that further endeared him to Tim and me. As I firmly pushed Chuck into the back seat of the radio car, his legs lashed out at me.

"You punk!" I yelled at him, slapping his legs back into the car.

A few minutes later, the paddy wagon arrived and transported Chuck to the Mission Station for processing. Once Chuck's crowd of teen thugs saw their leader going off in the wagon, they quickly dispersed. Chuck was booked for resisting arrest, carrying a concealed weapon, and assaulting a police office. Because he was a minor (although you couldn't tell by looking at him), Chuck was transported to the YGC (Youth Guidance Center) to await his hearing.

Within a few days, I received a notice to appear at the YGC for Chuck's hearing. I knew from previous experience these YGC proceedings were not as formal as traditional adult hearing. The hearing is overseen and conducted by a juvenile judge referred to as a "referee." In these cases, the referee acts as judge and jury.

When the case was called, I went into the hearing room and saw Chuck already sitting there, near an unkempt, unshaven man. (As it turned out, this was Chuck's father—the San Quentin alumnus.) The referee directed me to stand in front of the bench, and, seconds later, I was administered the oath.

That's when things started getting strange.

Right from the start, it was obvious the referee was hostile to me.

"Officer Petersen, I must tell you I'm very upset about this case," he said. "Did you really call the defendant a punk?"

"Yes," I responded, and the referee proceeded to chew my ass for the next several minutes, telling me how unprofessional I was.

But it was about to get worse.

"Officer Petersen," the referee said, "I direct you to apologize to Mr. Wright and to his father."

Without missing a beat, I looked the referee square in the eye and said, "I refuse to do that. Based on my knowledge of Chuck and my dealings with him, he definitely *is* a punk."

The referee blew his top. "That's it," he said, "I'm filing a report with the Chief of Police, recommending an un-officer-like conduct notation be placed in your personnel file. And I'm releasing Mr. Wright."

I was so pissed off I could barely see straight. But I knew I had to step back, clear my head, and act rationally. Which is exactly what I did.

In the spirit of covering my ass, I went directly to the Mission Station—even though it was my day off—and wrote a detailed report regarding this bullshit case. I marked it "Attention: Captain" and made damn sure a copy was sent to the Chief of Police's office.

I don't know whether my report saved me from reprimand. But one thing I do know: I never heard another thing about this matter. And a friend of mine in the personnel office told me nothing negative was ever put in my personnel file.

One post-script to this story:

The referee's behavior had been so strange and inexplicable to me that I looked into him. After conducting some private research, I discovered he was a left-wing partisan whose attitude seemed to be "hate the cop, love the criminal." And he did his very best to make cops' appearances before him as uncomfortable as possible.

Years later, when I decided to leave the police force, my number one reason for doing so was soft-on-crime "professionals" like that referee.

Don't Take My Husband!

While patrolling late one Saturday night in our radio car, Tim Thorsen and I suddenly heard loud screaming, origin unknown. Tim and I crossed the Harrison Street/24th Street intersection, and began training our sights on a nearby block, on which sat several apartment buildings.

We quickly determined the screaming was coming from one of several tiny apartments on that block. Just as we pulled over to the curb, an elderly Hispanic woman—a textbook Latin grandma type—ran over to our patrol car and screamed very excitedly, "A woman is being beaten! Come quickly with me! I'll show you where!"

We jumped out of the car and followed the woman up a nearby apartment staircase.

"There!" the woman gasped, pointing up to one of the units on the second floor. As soon as she said that, we could hear muffled noises coming from inside the apartment.

The apartment door was closed, so I began banging on it.

"Police!" I shouted. "Open up!"

After long, tense seconds, the door finally opened. Standing before us was a weeping young Hispanic woman, carrying a small, crying, five-year-old boy who clung to the woman's torn nightgown. The woman was bleeding from her mouth and nose. Her face was very swollen, her eyes almost shut.

"Come in," the young woman said softly, through her tears. We walked past her into an apartment that was very neat and tidy—except in the kitchen, which undoubtedly was the scene of the altercation. On the kitchen table—not far from a crucifix on the wall—sat the woman's husband, dressed in nothing but a T-shirt and boxer shorts. By the looks of him, the woman had landed a few good punches of her own. The man's lip and shoulder were bloody.

In very broken English, the woman mumbled, "My husband and I . . . We had fight. He was hitting me."

Tim and I separated the woman and her husband and attempted to ascertain what had happened. Because Tim had been in the Marine Corps and later went to seminary, he was good in these kinds of situations. His interrogation style was gentle yet firm. And it didn't take us long to determine we had encountered a typical domestic dispute—one fueled by too many beers.

"Look," I said after we had brought the husband and wife back together into the kitchen, "you're both in trouble. But we can help you get out of this trouble, if you'll leave for the night," I said, pointing to the husband. (We could not arrest him for assault, because his wife refused to press charges.)

As soon as I suggested the husband leave for the night, he went crazy.

"I no leave my home! No way!" he screamed, lashing out at Tim and me. As he grabbed for Tim, I jumped him. The next thing I knew, the woman was attacking me from behind with a wooden folding chair. The sharp blow across my back sent me crashing to the kitchen floor.

And then it got worse.

In the next split-second, the five-year old child, who previously had been clinging like a baby to his mother, jumped from his mother's arms and started kicking me as I attempted to get off the floor.

"Don't take my husband!" the woman shrieked. "Don't take him! He is a good man and I make him mad! So he hit me!"

Sadly—at least in her world—that was perfectly normal and acceptable.

Rather than calling Child Protective Services and/or arresting the woman for assault on a police officer, we elected to arrest the husband for simple drunkenness. Our thinking was, *If we handle it that way, at least the fight will be over for the rest of the night. And everyone will be safe for the moment.*

Besides, experience told us there really was nothing else to do.

The woman—sadly, tragically, and like many other women in Hispanic culture—would never file charges against her abusive husband. She was too terrified of losing his support. So the beatings might continue for a lifetime.

And that was that.

Psych Duty

One assignment most police officers were not prepared for was a shift at the psych ward (Ward 92 at world-renowned San Francisco General Hospital). Part of the reason for this was a lack of training due to a lack of money. In general, the powers that be in San Francisco felt such things as transportation and education should be budget priorities. Training cops to deal effectively with emotionally or psychologically distressed people was barely on anyone's radar screen.

Since many police encounters involve engagement with emotionally disturbed people, cops often are looked upon to handle psych cases until a final diagnosis is rendered. This was especially true in San Francisco, because of the city's ability to attract musicians, artists, theatre people, homeless people, and others disproportionately susceptible to psychological distress—or to suicide.

Ward 92 housed patients clinically determined to be of potential danger to themselves or others. For the patients detained because of a police incident, a police guard (in plain clothes) was required as long as they were confined. This meant—believe it or not—the officer had to be in the psyche ward, behind locked doors, with virtually no means of defending himself or herself because guns were strictly prohibited.

Many times a police officer—myself included—would find himself guarding one particular patient because of the person's involvement in a police incident, but also guarding several other patients who had *no* police connection. One saving grace was restraints were placed on patients known to be violent. But otherwise you were on your own.

This made for an interesting—sometimes deeply troubling—experience. For your entire eight-hour shift, you shared space with people who believed they were from Mars . . . who saw green men . . . who communicated with dead loved ones . . . or who—quite rationally and soberly—were trying to figure out how to escape. The one piece of advice I was offered before I did psyche duty the first time was: *Always keep one eye open and never turn your back.*

Another serious problem was we were not medically trained to handle these patients. We were left to our own devices. This was made things extremely challenging and difficult because, in most cases, these people were sick and you didn't want to hurt them— even if they were attacking you or otherwise abusing you. The only back-up you had was from professional attendants locked on the other side of the holding room, separated from us by a very thick glass wall. Even if it only took them seconds to recognize you needed emergency assistance, it would feel like a lifetime.

Needless to say, psych duty did not top anyone's list of "choice assignments." I eventually was assigned there about ten times in my first three or four years on the police force. And I was always deeply relieved when those shifts were over.

The San Francisco Police Youth Fishing Program

One thing I was always proud of was the work done by the Police Athletic League (P.A.L.) on behalf of San Francisco's youth. Thanks to the police department, the youth of San Francisco benefited from organized baseball and basketball leagues, which, as an extra bonus, helped cultivate better relationships between the city's cops and youth—particularly underprivileged youth.

Starting in the summer of 1968, those programs were complemented by an innovative new program that still functions very successfully to this day, the Youth Fishing Program.

I remember how the program started. A number of officers got together and came up with the idea: to try to help youth have a proper perspective on the police, while having fun and building friendships with them. The cops particularly tried to recruit kids from the ghetto, promoting and organizing their efforts through schools and neighborhood parks. Everything by the police was done off-duty, so all the cops involved were volunteering their time. The vision was that the program would someday develop into something like Big Brothers of America.

There were two officers— John Mikulin and Frank Watts— who particularly helped launch the program. Both officers worked primarily in Chinatown, where (as I've previously mentioned) it was especially difficult to foster positive relationships between the police and citizens, because of the many cultural differences. The two officers who launched the program were, specifically, beat officers in Chinatown—professional partners and good friends— and both spoke various dialects of Chinese.

The officers did a superb job selling the program in the Chinese community and elsewhere, and almost immediately the four or five borrowed boats started filling with ten or twelve laughing kids each, all accompanied by one or two police officers. Soon, the San

Francisco Fishing Boats Association was actively participating, as well, lending boats for two- or three-hour trips a couple of times a week.

The fishing trips took place not only on the weekend, but often during the week, as well. I was lucky enough to participate in the program, going along several times as a deep-sea-fishing helper. We'd go out beyond the Golden Gate Bridge, where the waters were often choppy. But none of us minded. In fact, it seemed like the choppy waters just made things more fun.

As word spread about the program, more and more cops stepped up to volunteer. They'd heard guys like me say how fun and rewarding it was!

Now—more than forty-five years after the San Francisco Police Youth Fishing Program first began—it is still a major recreational opportunity for Bay Area youngsters. More than 130,000 boys and girls have participated in the program since its inception, allowing tens of thousands of kids the thrill of catching their first king salmon or striped bass. For most of those kids, it was their first-ever opportunity to sail under the Golden Gate Bridge and to go out into deep waters.

Due to the huge success of the program, private donations and corporate sponsorships have developed over the years. While the San Francisco Police Department provides the personnel, the actual costs of running the program come from the limited fundraising conducted by members of the program. Over the years the program also has partnered with organizations such as the Guardsmen and the San Francisco Police Officers Association. Many San Francisco businesses have sponsored a fishing trip for local youth, and sent along a representative to join the kids during their big adventure.

To further assist with the funding, the Fisherman's Wharf Merchants Association adopted the Youth Fishing Program as one of its "community partners." Member donations and a portion of the proceeds from the association's Annual Crab Feed Fundraiser go directly to the program.

Youth Fishing Program activities always have been provided at no cost to either the individual youngster or the organizations or groups they belong to. And the San Francisco Police Department is committed to keeping it that way.

In the chapters that follow, I'll discuss the various reasons why I ultimately left the police department. Generally when you leave a situation, it's because the "minuses" have outweighed the "plusses." But participating in the Youth Fishing Program was a huge plus for me (and countless other officers), and I'll always be grateful for that unique opportunity to help mentor San Francisco's youth.

Where are the Rest of Ya?

Tim Thorsen was off one Saturday so a beat man, Ken DeBrunner, was assigned to ride with me. We were on the 4 p.m. to midnight watch, assigned to my regular car, Mission 4.

Ken was a seventeen-year veteran of the police department whose recent years had been spent walking the beats. He was very low-key, quiet, and practical. His motto seemed to be, *Never rock the boat.* As he told me many times, "I just want to get my twenty years in, and then I'm out of here."

On this particular day, Ken was just coming back from back surgery and that concerned me.

"I'm worried they've returned you to the field too soon," I told Ken.

"Aw, we should be fine," Ken replied in his easygoing way. "Let's just make it our goal to get through this watch without incident."

Unfortunately, that was not to be.

At around 4:30 p.m. Ken and I were stopped at the red light at 22nd and Valencia. Suddenly the afternoon calm was broken by an urgent radio dispatch.

"Any Mission cars . . . Mission 4 . . . a report of 418 at the Northern Club . . . 22nd and Valencia . . . Code 2 (get there ASAP)."

"Mission 4, 10-4," we shot back, and within seconds I was pulling up to the curb in front of the Northern Club. As I killed the engine, Ken and I shot puzzled glances at each other. The Northern Club was a clean, respectable, quiet neighborhood bar that almost never experienced any trouble. What had changed?

Ken and I cautiously approached the front door of the club. As we pulled it open, we saw two bodies lying on the floor on their backs. To our left, we saw the bartender sticking his hand up from behind the bar, pointing excitedly to the rear of the club. We swung around, focusing our eyes on the back of the room.

Standing there was an absolutely enormous man. A wide, crazy grin was splashed across his face and in his right hand he was holding a barstool—waving it around like some kind of baton.

Ken and I took a couple of tentative steps toward the man, at which point he cocked his head and caught sight of us. Letting go of a loud belly laugh, he yelled, "Ha-ha!!! Where are the rest of ya? It's gonna take more than the two of you candy asses!"

Ken and I looked at each other and, without a word, backed out of the bar. Because of Ken's bad back, I knew I needed additional back-up. I walked briskly to our car and radioed for an ambulance, a paddy wagon, and any available back-up cars. I advised the dispatcher we were dealing with an in-progress 419 (fight with weapons).

Within minutes, another Mission car rolled up to help. John Mindermann and Jim Mancuso jumped out and, seconds later, the ambulance and paddy wagon arrived.

Now the situation seemed more in our favor. We now had six police officers at the scene, not counting the ambulance crew. I quickly explained to the new arrivals what Ken and I had just witnessed.

"There's a huge guy in there—in the back of the bar," I told them. "This guy thinks he's The Incredible Hulk or something. He's waving around a barstool like it's light as a feather. When Ken and I approached him, he went into full-blown taunting mode. Looks like he's primed for a cop fight."

We six cops quickly moved back into the bar. The Incredible Hulk wannabe had not moved, and began waving the barstool again, yelling, "That's more like it! *Now* we're gonna have some fun!"

The six of us spread out and began to circle our suspect. In the meantime, the ambulance crew came in behind us, to attempt to care for the injured men lying on the floor. As we got nearer our guy, he again began laughing like a certified maniac—then charged us. Instinctively, all of us jumped him at the same time. After a fistfight that seemed to last forever, we finally got him to the ground and on his stomach. I pulled his huge arms behind his back and attempted to handcuff him. But that wasn't easy. His hands, wrists, and forearms were so huge, we had to use several pairs of cuffs, linked together, to secure him. And even after we did so, he kept rolling around on the floor like a lunatic before we finally subdued him.

All of us were huffing and puffing from the tremendous fight as we escorted the suspect out the door, toward the paddy wagon.

But now we had another problem.

After catching his breath for a moment, the huge suspect still was maniacally resisting arrest. He jumped around and screamed as we brought him out the door. He jumped around and screamed as we attempted to shove him through the open door of the old style, open-back paddy wagon.

We lifted the huge man up toward the door and began to stuff him into the wagon. When he was nearly inside the wagon himself, John Mindermann, who was a big, 6'2" man, said, "I'll get this jerk inside." With that, John grabbed the bar above the doorway like a trapeze artist and, with his feet, began to push the suspect further into the wagon.

Suddenly—without warning—the suspect grabbed John's legs and pulled him into the wagon. Now we had to extract John!

That's when we caught a break.

After mixing it up with John as best as he could, the huge suspect finally ran out of gas and collapsed from exhaustion. Luckily, John was okay and we were able to transport the suspect to city prison. He was booked on a variety of charges, including assault with a deadly weapon and resisting arrest. The two bar patrons were treated and released without serious injury.

In the heat of the battle, I had forgotten about Ken's back problem. ("So did I," Ken later told me, grinning.) But Ken realized he was very fortunate not to have re-injured his back. That night, as we reported off-duty, Ken told our platoon commander he would prefer not to work the radio cars again, at least until he felt stronger.

Several weeks later, I went to court to testify at the trial, which was at the Hall of Justice in Chinatown. And I actually had the opportunity to speak with the defendant. Now that he was sober and his bruises were healed, he certainly was a different man. He still was a bit arrogant, but mostly he was apologetic. I asked him about the incident.

"I'm a merchant seaman," he said, "and we'd just hit port that day. We'd been at sea for several months, and were looking for some fun. My idea of fun is to get plastered, get into a fight, and blow off steam. And I'm grateful to you and your boys. That was one of the best fights I was ever in. I'll always remember it."

The court found him guilty and ordered him to jail for several months, with a lengthy probation period. His idea of fun came at a serious cost to his freedom.

Testimonials

One of our frequent social activities was testimonial dinners given for police officers retiring or being promoted. The dinner would be open to anyone on the police force, not just those in certain stations. The location usually was a cop-friendly restaurant such as Joe's Club, Bruno's, the Inn-Justice, or a social hall.

To outsiders, these events would have seemed strange in one particular way: Generally there was a lot of drinking—and the drinking often led to brawls among the attendees.

That's right—police officers would go to testimonial dinners for police officers, then start fistfights with their fellow officers.

Why did such a seemingly strange thing happen—and happen quite *frequently*?

It's hard for me to say exactly. Sometimes a fistfight would be started by two cops who simply didn't like each other, whose mutual animosity was fueled by booze. Sometimes it would involve one cop wanting another cop's assignment and believing he deserved it.

But I think something larger was actually happening:

Given the enormous, unending stress of police work, I think the testimonial dinners were a pressure-release valve. Maybe the cops wailed on their fellow cops because, so often, they were restrained from behaving that way toward the citizens they encountered each day—citizens who might be calling them every name in the book, spitting on them, or suddenly assaulting them.

The thinking within police ranks seemed to be: *Maybe it's not a great thing that we cops are beating each other up at these dinners. But outside of an occasional bloody nose, nobody really gets hurt.* As strange as that may sound, it was accepted within San Francisco police culture.

The real danger came into play after the event. Despite drinking for several hours, most attendees felt they could drive home because they were pros or because someone "up there" was watching out for them.

One of my best friends on the police force believed this, too.

His name was Denny.

Denny was liked by everyone. He was a great cop, and a loving husband and father. Denny and I went through training together and, early in our careers, worked out of the same stations.

One night, after attending one of the police testimonial dinners (I was not in attendance), Denny's car flipped over while he was heading home. He was killed instantly.

The precise cause of Denny's accident was never determined, but it had an important impact on future police testimonial dinners. Testimonials subsequently were planned on a more formal basis, and became less frequent.

Perhaps Denny's untimely death was not in vain.

Ultimate Neglect

Tim and I were working the 4 p.m. to midnight watch out of Mission Station. We had just jumped into our cruiser when our radio came alive.

"Mission 4 . . . a 909x (interview a woman) . . . at 384 San Jose Avenue . . . Apartment 103."

I radioed back "Mission 4 . . . 10-4," and Tim and I gave each other a quick, knowing nod. We were being directed to go less than half a block from where we were. We actually could have walked to the location in a minute or two.

After driving the short distance, we stopped in front of 384 San Jose Avenue, Apartment 103, rang the bell, and seconds later were greeted by a very concerned-looking woman.

"Oh, officers. Thank you for coming." She told her name, then said, "I'm the manager of this apartment complex. I'm very concerned about the occupants of apartment ___, especially the children there. I've been hearing crying coming from that apartment. There are small children in there, and their parents aren't home. It's been going on for several days."

"How do you know the parents aren't home?" I asked.

"Someone told me. They said the little children are left completely alone for long stretches—maybe eight hours or more, I'm not sure—while the parents are working."

Tim and I, accompanied by the manager, went to the apartment and rang the bell. We could hear whimpering coming from within. No one responded to our ringing or knocking. Tim and I looked at each other.

"We've got reasonable cause to gain entry to this apartment," I said. "Ma'am, can we have the master key?"

"Absolutely," she said. She was carrying it, and quickly handed it to me. We all went inside.

The apartment was dark except for some late-afternoon sunlight coming through the shaded windows. It was a small, modest apartment: one bedroom with a kitchen and living room adjacent to the kitchen.

When our eyes adjusted to the dimly lit room, we saw the crib from which came the pitiful, whimpering noises. Walking quickly toward the crib, we could see the nearly lifeless bodies of two children.

We flicked on the light, and, in the next moment, saw something I'll never forget. It was two little boys, dressed in diapers although they obviously were too old to be in diapers. The boys were too weak to sit up on their own. And I immediately noticed another thing: the boys likely were even older than they at first seemed. Their heads were unusually large and out of proportion with the rest of their bodies.

"We need to call for an ambulance, Code 3," I said.

"And then a unit from the Juvenile Detail," Tim said somberly. I nodded and Tim radioed in.

The ambulance arrived within minutes, taking the two children to Mission Emergency Hospital. Then Tim and I began canvassing the apartment. It was modestly furnished, with a stale smell due to lack of ventilation. Permeating the entire apartment was the foul odor coming from the room where the children had been lying in their own waste.

One very odd thing I spotted was a stack of boxes in the corner of the living room. The boxes contained ladies' clothing from several major, upscale department stores. But it didn't appear any of the items ever had been worn. They still were neatly folded, exactly as they had come from the store. Another extremely unusual thing I observed was the apparent lack of food you would normally find in a home where children lived. No sign of Fruit Loops anywhere—except maybe the parents of these poor children.

"The mother and father should be home within a half hour or so," the manager told us, "if they stick to their usual schedule." She looked relieved that *finally* something was being done about this situation.

"Okay, we'll wait, then," Tim said. He gestured *outside* with his thumb and the three of us went out of the apartment to wait. After the manager went back to her office, Tim and I engaged in a mini-stakeout, standing across the courtyard from the apartment door, at a position where we could see anyone enter or exit.

About twenty minutes later, a man and woman appeared from around the corner, stood briefly outside the apartment door as the man extracted his key from his pocket, then went in.

As soon as we saw them, Tim and I walked briskly toward the apartment door, ringing the bell as soon as we got there. The door was quickly opened by two very startled people. They hadn't even had time to notice their children were gone.

"San Francisco police," I said curtly to the couple. "I'm officer Petersen; this is officer Thorsen. We're investigating you for child neglect."

Looking startled and confused, the woman said thickly, "Come in. Um . . . How can we help you?"

"Are you the mother and father of the two boys in this apartment?" I asked.

They both silently nodded.

"We have been here for an hour or so," I continued. "After responding to a call regarding your children. We were previously in your apartment, let in by the manager. Your boys have been taken to the hospital, and the juvenile inspectors are on their way here. They'll pick up the investigation."

"Whhhhhhhhat?" the man spat out. "How dare you! They're our children. You have no right to bust in here and take our boys."

"We'll see what the courts say about that," Tim said. Then I took a purposeful step toward both of them.

"You're both under arrest for violation of Section 602 of the Welfare and Institutions Code . . . child endangerment," I said. Tim and I immediately cuffed them. A short time later, the two inspectors from Juvenile arrived, and we turned the man and woman over to them.

As fathers ourselves, Tim and I found this case extremely distressing. We talked about it quietly as we headed over to Mission Emergency Hospital to check on the boys' condition.

"My God, Ray. Can you believe what we've just seen?" Tim asked.

"Like an absolute nightmare," I replied quietly. "Let's just hope those boys will be okay, after they get medical attention."

Tim silently nodded, and we said nothing else until we got to the hospital.

The head ER nurse at Mission Emergency, Cathy Crowley, was the wife of a fellow San Francisco police officer, and Tim and I knew her fairly well. After we arrived and parked, we immediately sought Cathy out and luckily were able to locate her quickly. She was shaking her head in anger and disbelief as we approached her. She didn't have to ask why we were there.

"This is easily one of the worst cases of child neglect I've seen in my eighteen years as a nurse," Cathy said. Just then, the attending doctor walked quickly up to Cathy, as she told him why we were there.

"It's really bad," the doctor said, shaking his head exactly as Cathy had. "The two boys are seriously dehydrated, in shock, and suffering from malnutrition. They're both covered with sores from head to toe."

"Have you been able to make a prognosis yet?" I asked.

"I'll tell you what I know so far," the doctor said. "In my judgment, from the looks of the boys, I believed they are severely underdeveloped. We don't yet have their actual ages, but I know they're underdeveloped. And I'll tell you something else," he said, pausing and looking first Tim and then me squarely in the eye. "If these boys had not been found today, they would have died within a few days. Or, at the very least, suffered irreversible brain damage. But still—given the damage that's already occurred, and that they arrived here such a short time ago—I can't yet say what they're facing long-term."

Several weeks later, Tim and I were summoned to Juvenile Court to testify at the custody hearing for the two boys. It was there we heard things that further appalled us—and made us question just who "the system" serves. The inspectors and District Attorney told us—to our great anger and dismay—that, after their hospital stay, the boys had been given back to their parents until the hearing. The Juvenile Officers blithely told us they had found no prior criminal record for either of the suspects—nor was there any evidence of prior child neglect charges having been filed. We were told, "Don't be surprised if the court decides to put the parents on probation, and allow the children to remain with their parents under the court's supervision."

Which is actually what happened.

One great irony in this case needs to be pointed out:

When we first had encountered the mother and father on that terrible day, they didn't appear to be monsters. On the contrary, they appeared to be a normal, hard-working couple. There was no sign of alcohol abuse, drug abuse, or addiction of any kind. In fact, they actually told us during that initial encounter, "We love our boys and are working hard to provide them with a good home."

Sadly—and shamefully—the court bought it.

Probably needless to say, Tim and I often talked about this case over the next few years. It haunted me for a long time—perhaps still does. Although I would remain on the police force years beyond this incident, it was cases such as this that ultimately would lead me to leave police work.

If the "system" wouldn't protect innocent victims like those little boys, who *would* it protect?

Keep Your Shirt On!

Saturday afternoon was not very busy on Valencia Street, since a lot of the businesses were closed. Parking was not a problem, either, so when Tim Thorsen and I spotted the double-parked Chevy—with a gang of tough guys gathered near it—we quickly pulled over.

Tim was driving and I was in the back seat with "Nails," an affable, benevolent, usually-homeless drunk reminiscent of Otis on *Andy of Mayberry*. We were transporting Nails to Mission Station for violation of 152MPC (public drunkenness). This wasn't the first time we'd thus chauffeured Nails to a place where he could dry out.

But we didn't mind. Nails, who was a former carpenter (hence his nickname), was a nice guy who tied one on once in a while. This was one of those times. Previously in the afternoon, the manager at Ted's Donuts had called us and said, "Nails came in a while ago, and now he's passed out. He's pissed his pants and can't walk without help. Can you guys come get him outa here?"

We dutifully complied.

For his own well-being, we decided to book Nails at Mission Station. Our thinking was, *At least there he'll be safe and get a couple of decent meals, as a guest of the city of San Francisco.*

So we were en route to Mission Station when we spotted the gang near the double-parked Chevy.

"Pull over," I said to Tim. "Looks like we need to check this out."

The gang clustered near the Chevy consisted of five or six young-adult males engaged in a very animated discussion. As we pulled up close to them, they arrogantly chose to ignore our presence.

I rolled down the window and yelled out, "Hey, does this car belong to one of you guys?"

No response.

I yelled again—still no reaction.

Finally, one of the guys yelled back, "Yeah, yeah . . . Keep your shirt on!"

When I heard that, I made sure Nails was secured, then immediately jumped out of the car. "I'll see what this jerk's problem is," I said to Tim. I walked up to the gang and stood in front of them. To my left was the guy who had yelled back at us.

"Are you the owner of this double-parked Chevy?" I asked him.

"Yeah," he grunted arrogantly. The guy was obviously a real intellectual.

"Then let me see your driver's license," I shot back. In a flash, The Jerk's right fist was careening toward the left side of my face. I did a pull-back motion worthy of Mohammed Ali, and the blow merely glanced off my left shoulder. Without missing a beat, The Jerk bolted down Valencia Street, with yours truly in hot pursuit.

As I started gaining on him, both of us began to tumble. All I could think of was *Man, if I fall and he gets on top of me, it'll be a bitch getting up, with all the crap we have to carry in our uniform.*

I must have jinxed myself by thinking that, because the next second I was falling. As I barreled into the ground, I did a nifty tuck-and-roll movement and bounced up on my feet. The Jerk was up against a building, coming to his feet. With my left hand I grabbed him by the collar and, with my right hand, cracked him over the head with my nightstick. He dropped like a rock, started bleeding from the head, and I immediately handcuffed him.

In the meantime, Tim was juggling double-duty. He had to stay with our prisoner, Nails, and also call for assistance so we could secure The Jerk's friends. Tim did both things beautifully. After they saw what happened to their buddy, the "tough guys" readily dispersed. They didn't want any of that action.

But the peace lasted only a few seconds. Now cuffed and coming out of his daze, The Jerk started yelling at me, "You motherfucker! I'll get you! I'll kick your fuckin' ass!"

Luckily for my abused ears, the Mission Station paddy wagon rolled up seconds later, to take The Jerk to Mission Emergency

Hospital to—you might say—have his head examined. That had become necessary after he met my reliable nightstick.

As I angrily put him into the paddy wagon, I spat out, "Looks like your ass is mine, you prick!" He gave me a foul look as the wagon doors slammed behind him. He was soon treated at the hospital, then transported to Mission Station for booking.

Meanwhile, Tim, Nails, and I headed to Mission Station, where we got Nails booked and secured. As I was placing Nails in his cell, he turned to me and said, "Man, I never want to get *you* pissed off."

I smirked at Nails as the booking sergeant shouted out to me, "Ray, you've got a call from Inspector Sergeant Brown at Room 105 (Inspector's Headquarters). He says call him ASAP."

I walked over to a nearby phone and rang Inspector Sergeant Brown.

"Room 105, Brown here," the Inspector said gruffly.

"This is Officer Petersen," I said. "I was told to call you."

"Yeah, Ray" he said. "Thanks for returning my call so quickly. I'm calling about my nephew." In the next few moments, I learned his nephew was The Jerk from the Valencia Street incident. "Can you fill me in on what happened?" Inspector Sergeant Brown asked.

After hearing my account of what took place—including my cracking his nephew over the head with my nightstick—he actually *thanked* me.

"Ray," he said, "unfortunately, my nephew considers himself a real badass. And it's brought him a helluva lot of trouble in his life. He just received a dishonorable discharge from the Marine Corps for beating one of the men in his company. But as many fights as he's gotten into, until today he's never been put down. And I hope he thinks about that for a long time. As far as I'm concerned, he can sit in jail for as long as it takes for him to wise up. Hopefully, you've done him a real service. Anyway . . . thanks again."

Tim and I went to the business office to complete our report. As we finished up, Inspector Sergeant Brown's nephew was brought in to be booked. He was wearing a big bandage around his head and was sporting a black eye. The list of charges against him was read, but he never made a peep.

As we placed him in his cell, he looked at Tim and me and said, "I'm sorry, officers."

"Next time, you'll think twice before taking a swing at a cop," I said.

Inspector Sergeant Brown's nephew pled guilty to the charges and later received a sentence of a few months in the county jail, plus a rather long probation.

I never heard from Inspector Sergeant Brown again.

Shots Rang Out

Patrolman Tim Thorsen and I were working the midnight to 8 a.m. watch out of the Mission Station. I liked Tim a lot, and always felt we complemented each other well. Tim was an ex-Marine and a devoutly religious Catholic. He even had had aspirations, at one point, of becoming a priest. But I knew him as a happily married father of five. If you were going to be working a beat with another police officer, Tim was the kind of guy you wanted to be with. He was rock-solid and a genuinely impressive person. In fact, he ultimately became Deputy Chief of the Department.

This particular night, Tim and I were assigned the Mission 4 car (D-4). It was around 4 a.m. and we were parked in the Richfield Gas Station at 14th and Mission Streets, casually talking with the night manager. Suddenly the early-morning calm was shattered by exploding firecrackers.

Or was it gun shots?

In a moment, all our senses shot to life. Seconds later, we saw one of the strangest, most potentially deadly scenes I'd ever witnessed. Our patrol car was facing out toward Mission Street and—right in front of us—a car suddenly cruised by, slowly heading south. The grubby-looking male driver was hanging out the window, hurling curses at someone on the sidewalk and shooting what appeared to be a rifle. His equally-grubby-looking female passenger was leaning over, toward the driver. We couldn't tell what she was doing, but it appeared she was guiding the steering wheel as the man trained his rifle out the car.

The suspects had no idea they were doing this right in front of two cops.

Shots rang out, as the male assailant trained his rifle on a sidewalk pedestrian. In the next milli-second, we saw the intended target—a man desperately running south down the Mission Street sidewalk to try to avoid being peppered by bullets.

Tim flashed the red light on and hit the siren. He shot the radio car out of the service station and quickly got behind the suspects' vehicle.

In a flash the driver jumped out of his car with his rifle, still spraying the sidewalk with bullets. Tim screamed our car to a halt, and was attempting to get out of the car, when the suspect turned his attention on us—and on Tim in particular.

I bolted out of the car and drew my gun, pointing it lethally at the armed suspect.

"Drop the gun—right now!!!" I screamed. Then I turned my attention to the female passenger.

"Get out of the car! Get on the ground! Now!" I yelled.

The male suspect hesitated and turned toward his intended victim. I cocked my weapon and prepared to fire.

"Drop the gun!!!" I screamed again. The suspect turned back toward Tim. I took aim and was about to pull the trigger, when suddenly the suspect dropped his rifle and put his hands in the air.

Then something very strange happened.

As the suspect dropped his rifle, it discharged. The victim—who ran toward the suspect when he put his hands in the air—suddenly was struck by the bullet. He was hit in the lower left leg—almost immediately crashing to the ground from his wound.

How bizarre, I thought. *This guy was never struck when he was a sitting duck on the sidewalk. And now he gets shot when the assailant drops his weapon?*

Tim and I cuffed the assailant and his female passenger and placed them under arrest. We radioed in for an ambulance, and the victim was taken to Mission Emergency Hospital, where he was treated for a minor gunshot wound.

Tim and I finished the crime scene investigation and interviewed the suspects and the victim. All three were familiar to the San Francisco police department. All had lengthy rap sheets, including convictions for assault, burglary, drugs, and stolen autos. These people weren't exactly pillars of the community.

But what was <u>this</u> strange incident about?

We soon found out:

It turns out, the assailant and woman passenger were lovers. The "victim" was the woman's husband. Earlier in the night, he had attempted to gun down the male driver, and now the two lovers were seeking revenge. (They knew the husband often was out on Mission Street late at night, on foot.) The woman's role included loading the rifle and—just as we thought we'd observed—holding the car's steering wheel while the suspect leaned out the window to shoot at her husband.

All three people were booked—two for attempted murder and the husband for an outstanding warrant. Because of their previous incarceration—the two men were "graduates" of San Quentin Prison and the woman had served time in the county jail—they got the book thrown at them. The men were ultimately sentenced to life in prison and the woman to fifteen-to-thirty years.

This incident has an interesting post-script—one I'm very proud of:

Based on the events of that night—and Tim's and my response as police officers—police brass determined lives had been saved. In recognition of this, Tim and I each received from the Chief of Police a Meritorious Award for "Outstanding Bravery in the Performance of Police Duty."

We each accepted the award proudly and gratefully.

A special note: Tim and his wife later became godparents to one of our sons.

ACCIDENT INVESTIGATION BUREAU STORIES

After I was with the police force about a year, I requested a transfer to the Accident Investigation Bureau, or AIB, as it was commonly known. Ever since I could remember—dating all the way back to conversations I'd had with cops when I still was working in my dad's butcher shop—I'd been told "the AIB is the place to be." That was what you really needed to shoot for, everyone told me.

This "word on the street" was reinforced big-time once I got onto the San Francisco police force. The constant buzz was, *If you can get into the AIB, that's the best uniform job you can get around here.*

And the buzz wasn't lying.

The AIB simply offered you a lot more freedom. You could cruise the whole city; you no longer were restricted to just one section, as I had been at Richmond Station and Mission Station. An accident could happen anywhere in the city ("And it generally does," we used to laugh.) There were only six or eight teams that made up the AIB, so you had a lot of space to roam around in, a lot of ground to cover.

As a young, "pumped-up" cop, I loved the "open spaces" idea of the AIB. It gave you a lot of fast-breaking incidents to immerse yourself into, and a lot of situations that forcibly tested your ability to perform in the face of grave danger or chaos.

And AIB cops rose to the occasion.

During the time when I was with the AIB, more meritorious conduct awards went to AIB cops than to any other type in the city. I could clearly see AIB cops had the talent and drive to perform at a very high level—and I hungered to be part of that action.

123

That's why I had wasted no time getting myself put on the AIB Transfer List. I wanted to be considered just as soon as an AIB position opened up.

As luck would have it, I didn't have to wait long.

Not long after my first anniversary on the force, on a Saturday, I received a call at home from Mission Station.

"Ray, when you come in next time, the lieutenant wants to see you. A transfer memo has come down," I was told.

It was a Saturday, and I was supposed to be off, but I couldn't wait. I made a beeline for the station.

When I got there about an hour later, they told me to go into the Watch Commander's office. As I entered, he waved me to sit down and said, "Ray, I just wanted to congratulate you. You've received that transfer to the Traffic Bureau you requested. You're to report first thing Monday morning to Captain Kiley."

On Monday morning, Captain Kiley swore me in.

"By the way, Ray," he said after the brief ceremony was over, "I've known your Uncle Ray for years. If you become half as good a cop as he is, I'll be one very happy commander."

This Could Have Been Ugly

My partner Bill was off, and I was working the 2 to 10 p.m. watch in the car designated Traffic 2. Around 5:30 p.m., an all-cars broadcast crackled over the radio:

"Any southern car . . . central car . . . or northern car . . . a 415 at 7th and Market Streets . . . A report of motorcycles on the sidewalk in front of Walgreens Drug Store."

I didn't initially respond, because this kind of situation wasn't something AIB typically dealt with.

The radio barked again.

"Any car . . . any traffic car . . . Traffic 2, what's your 10-20?"

I swiftly picked up and shot back, "This is Traffic 2. I'm in the Twin Peaks area."

Communications called back, "Traffic 2 . . . respond to Market and 7th Street. We'll try to raise back-up."

"10-4," I responded, and gunned the cruiser toward my destination.

It took about ten minutes to arrive at the corner of 7th and Market Street. As I sped up to the curb, I noticed a large crowd gathered in front of Walgreen's Drug Store. Several people ran over to my car and started yelling at me in very agitated tones, "The Hell's Angels are taking over the street! They're taking over the entire street!"

I could see several motorcycles illegally parked on the sidewalk outside Walgreen's. But their riders were just sitting on them, bantering with the crowd. Nothing seemed threatening or out-of-hand, but I still had an odd feeling about the scene. Before jumping out of my car, I tight-fisted the radio and called in, "Traffic 2 . . . on scene and need back-up."

A few seconds later the radio crackled on the dashboard.

"10-4, Traffic 2. Solo motorcycle officers are en route."

With that, I shot out of the cruiser and started walking toward the bikers. As I did so, they looked at me and started to laugh arrogantly in my face.

"I smell burnt bacon—must be a pig around!" one of them spat out. As I drew closer, he snarled at me, "Where's the rest of the Keystone Cops?"

I gave him my best Clint Eastwood glare and said, "I don't need any help. All the help I need is right here." I patted my holstered .357 magnum.

That mostly shut him up, and after a few more unpleasantries were exchanged, I managed to convince the Hell's Angels it would be in their best interest to get on their bikes and proceed to the Hall of Justice (with which they were very familiar), so we could bring this episode to a close. I confiscated each of their driver's licenses and followed them in my cruiser to the Hall. It was a Hell's Angel Parade—with Officer Petersen as the enforcement caboose. The whole thing made me feel like Sergeant York or something.

Within minutes we arrived at the Hall of Justice, and gathered in the briefing room. I advised the Hell's Angels they were going to be cited for reckless driving, and that any outstanding warrants against them would be executed. A warrant check was made on all six of the Angels, which led to the discovery that three had outstanding traffic warrants. We proceeded to deal with them right then and there.

In all, six citations were given and the bikers were released. As they were leaving, one of them came over to me and said, "The reason we didn't give you a hard time was you treated us decently. And you seemed *very* serious when you patted your gun."

A .357 magnum is a great equalizer.

It's Not Worth Losing Your Head

It was a dreary, rainy day in early April. I was on patrol in Traffic 3 and suddenly the dashboard lit up with an urgent call:

"All cars . . . hot chase in progress . . . station car from the Potrero in pursuit of vehicle heading north on Third Street, towards the downtown area."

My hand shot out toward the radio, but paused as another urgent call came rapidly across.

"All cars . . . Code 4 (chase is over) . . . requesting fire trucks and ambulance at Third and Berry Streets."

What in the world had just happened?

First, we're told there's a "hot chase" in progress.

Seconds later, we're told it's over.

Seconds after that . . . fire trucks and ambulance being summoned?

One thing was obvious—this wasn't going to be pretty.

The dashboard radio lit up a third time. With a call directed squarely at me.

"Traffic 3 . . . respond to Third and Berry . . . 519 (injury accident) . . . possibly fatal . . . ambulance and fire department on the way."

I smashed the pedal to the metal and shot toward Third and Berry. As I screamed up to the curb, I saw a horrific sight: the fire department attempting to extinguish a huge ball of fire leaping from gas-station pumps at the corner.

I shot out of the cruiser and warily approached the conflagration. All I could see was what was left of a car, flames shooting out of it as it rested on top of gas pumps.

"We think there's three people caught in the car!" a station officer bellowed at me as I ran up. He kept shouting at me, to be heard above the chaos. "The car was reported stolen! It may have been involved in a 211 (hold-up)! We have eyewitnesses in the

Candlestick Park area who saw the vehicle stolen and called this in. That's when the chase started."

Soon other police officers gathered—like ghosts coming out of nowhere—and I started hearing additional crime-scene details.

"The suspect car was heading up Third Street at a very high rate of speed," one of them said, as the flames continued their mad dance behind him. "It crossed over the channel bridge—a steel drawbridge—which was very slippery. The construction has heavy steel grates on the roadbed, and heavy steel crossbeams on the sides, to protect the main structure of the bridge. The suspect's car evidently hit those steel grates and started to slide out of control. The side of the car hit the crossbeams and spun several hundred feet into the gas station, where it exploded upon impact with the gas pumps."

The fire department worked feverishly to get the flames under control. Within twenty or thirty minutes, they had done so. It was only then that the scene revealed its most horrifying secrets.

From what we could see, there were three people in the car—but no survivors.

But things soon became even more horrifying.

As we began conducting a thorough investigation—measuring, taking photos, looking for eyewitnesses—one of the responding firemen shot me a dead-serious glance and waved me over.

"I need to let you know," he said, "one of the victims is not totally in the car."

"What do you mean, not totally in the car?" I asked.

He looked like he'd seen a ghost and was not able to speak for a moment.

"We just put this together—what happened," he said. "He's not totally in the car, because he was leaning out the window when the car impacted the crossbeam on the bridge. He was decapitated when his head was caught in the steel crossbeams on the bridge. It's still impaled on the bridge."

I don't remember what I said or did in response. I think I was too dazed.

The coroner was called to the scene, and took charge of the remains, including the head on the bridge and its owner in the car.

Even he wasn't prepared for a scene that grisly.

Now I Lay Me Down

John Minoli and I were in the Squad Room getting our briefing prior to our 2 to 10 p.m. tour of duty. Sgt. Ed Cosgrove came in and beckoned us out into the hall. Ed was a senior patrolman, a sergeant, about sixty years old, and one of my supervising officers. Ed would advise us as to accident situations we had to respond to, especially those involving significant traffic tie-ups. On this particular day, Ed advised us there was a serious accident in our beat area, and we were to respond.

En route to the scene, John and I were informed the ambulance on the scene had requested the coroner to respond; the alleged victim was 802—dead.

Upon arrival at the scene, Pier 41 on the Embarcadero, we rapidly made our way through fire trucks, radio cars, ambulances, and the normal truck traffic one would find at this time of day on the waterfront. The ambulance steward directed us to the victim.

"It's an apparent suicide," he said. "That's not official yet, but that's definitely what it looks like."

Then we saw something I'll never forget.

It was the body of an older man, very well-dressed and well-groomed, lying face down near the right rear wheels of an 18-wheel tractor/trailer rig.

What the witnesses soon told us was even more chilling. One of them stated, "I saw this man standing near the rear wheels while the truck was parked. The truck driver initially was outside the truck, but he didn't see the man."

The witness was shaken and had to pause for a moment to gather himself. Then he went on.

"When the truck driver got into the cab and started the truck, the man suddenly lay down and positioned his head under the wheel as the truck pulled out. I watched in horror as the man's head was smashed like a melon—like it had been dropped from a building. It was horrifying."

Based on this eyewitness account and others, we quickly concluded death had been instantaneous.

To make the situation even more chilling, it appeared to John and me the victim had dressed for the occasion. He looked as if he were going to a wedding or a high-level business meeting.

John and I searched the body before the coroner took it away. Fortunately for us, the man had put his wallet into his well-pressed suit, and we quickly discovered his identity.

Shortly thereafter, we drove to the address listed on the victim's ID. The man had lived in a ratty, run-down apartment building on Eddy Street, in a marginal part of the Tenderloin that once had been a notorious part of the city's red-light district.

As we came in through the front door, we immediately spotted the apartment manager.

"Is one of your tenants named _____ ?" we asked. "He's an older gentleman." We rattled off a cursory description of the man.

"Yes, he lives here," the apartment manager responded. "Has for many years, as a matter of fact. What's going on? What's wrong?"

"Mr. _____ was just found dead," I said. "Apparent suicide. We're investigating."

The expression on the apartment manager's face was a strange mix of *I'm terribly sorry to hear of his death* and *I don't want to be involved in this situation.* We told him we needed access to Mr. _____'s apartment, and he let us in.

The apartment was a tiny studio. It had very little furniture, but was extremely clean and neat as a pin. Mr. _____ obviously had been a "neat freak."

As we wandered around the apartment, looking for any clues as to why the man had tragically taken his own life, additional details emerged about him. The apartment manager told us, "He was a loner. Kept to himself. Never caused any trouble. Always thought it was strange that he lived here, although I know it's close to where he worked before he retired. It still was strange, though.

You wouldn't figure a classy guy like that would be interested in living near the Tenderloin. Maybe it was just his world."

We asked the apartment manager if he'd seen Mr. _____ earlier that day.

"Yup, I did. I remember why he was so dressed up, what the occasion was. That was it, though. Not much else to tell."

John and I scoured the tiny apartment for a suicide note or anything else that might offer a clue as to why Mr. _____ had come to this end. We found no note, but did find evidence Mr. _____ had a family.

Perhaps he just missed them terribly?

Perhaps he couldn't see them for some reason?

We were left with nothing but speculation.

 Soon the coroner's deputy and driver arrived. The information John and I had gathered was turned over to the coroner's office, and the coroner's deputy took charge from that point on.

Several weeks later, an inquest was held by the coroner to ascertain the official cause of death. He determined there was no evidence of foul play. The investigation also, by this point, had obtained information from Mr. _____ 's family that he had shown signs of depression and actually discussed taking his own life.

The official finding was death by suicide.

Case closed.

Or as "closed" as something like this ever can be.

Unexpected Climb

John Minoli and I were patrolling the Richmond District in the car dubbed Traffic 13. This part of the District was mostly residential, with multi-bedroom family homes dotting its landscape, adjacent to Golden Gate Park. It was a pleasant part of the city, teeming with tourists in the summer and close to the naval base on Treasure Island.

As we cruised along, the midday calm suddenly was shattered by two pedestrians—Klaas van der Weg and his sister Helen—desperately flagging us down at 33rd Avenue.

"We just saw two guys fall off a cliff!" Klaus yelled. He looked extremely agitated and upset. "It happened over by the Palace of Legion of Honor!"

"Please follow us!" Helen shouted, trying to hold back tears. "We'll show you where!"

We quickly followed the distraught brother and sister to the scene.

As we arrived at the top of the nearly cliff, John and I saw twenty-year-old Dan Shelhart and nineteen-year-old Tim Myers—both, we later found out, attending naval training on Treasure Island—desperately clinging to the side of a sheer cliff below us, approximately 150 feet from our vantage point. Being young naval hot-shots and way over-confident about their ability to be Batman and Robin, they'd tried to descend the steep, jagged cliff as a short-cut to the beach far below.

As John and I took in the sight, we turned and looked at each other, shaking our heads. White-foamed waves endlessly pounded the jagged rocks below.

At that point, one of the stranded would-be climbers shouted out to us.

"There are actually three of us!" Dan called out. "Our friend is down there, lying on the beach! He fell off the cliff and is injured!"

John ran back to the cruiser and called in for fire department and ambulance support. He was told they'd be there ASAP.

But I knew we couldn't wait.

"We gotta go after the injured guy right now," I said to John.

"Roger," John said. "Let's do it."

We gingerly started descended the steep cliff, trying to reach the injured party.

But no dice. As we got to closer to the victim, we could see we couldn't reach him, despite that he was only a few feet away. To get to him would have meant swimming around to the cove where he was lying. The rough, choppy water and rising tide totally prevented that.

Just then, deafening sirens pealed through the day as we saw the fire department arriving. It was battalion #7 directed by Chief Gemignani.

"Nice going," John muttered admiringly. "Man, they got here in a heartbeat."

John and I went to assist the firefighters in pulling Dan and Tim to safety.

Two out of three, I thought, *but we've still got that injured guy down on the beach.*

Fortunately, that's when The Hero on the White Horse arrived, in the form of a U.S. Coast Guard helicopter. Despite the winds buffeting the cliff area and choppy waters crashing all around, the chopper expertly landed, quickly brought the victim aboard, and flew him over to the Naval Hospital at 15th Avenue and Lake Street.

Tim and Dan had to pay the piper a bit sooner. Thanks to their woeful inability to descend the cliff, their bodies were riddled with abrasions and contusions. And they might be facing military disciplinary actions for pulling such as stunt. They were transported to Richmond Station and turned over to the Armed Services Police.

A Mother's Nightmare

Bill and I were in the roll-call room being briefed prior to starting the 2 to 10 p.m. watch. We were assigned our usual car, Traffic 2. Suddenly the desk duty officers came in and told us we had a Code 3 (red light, siren) that appeared very serious, a possible "fatal."

The accident had taken place in the projects near Candlestick Park (where a ballgame was going on), about ten minutes from the Hall of Justice. As we headed to the scene—siren screaming, red light flashing—the radio lit up with further details:

"Ambulance and officers now on the scene . . . taking the victim to M.E.H (Mission Emergency Hospital . . . condition of the victim critical."

As we arrived, we came upon a shocking, unforgettable sight. A large crowd of people—most of them African-Americans woefully crying—stood on the sidewalk, near where the accident had taken place. A man rushed forward and directed us to one lady in particular, the victim's mother, who was sobbing inconsolably.

"The little girl who got hit . . . it was her daughter," the man told us. "Poor little thing is just six years old."

Meanwhile, the driver of the car—a middle-aged white man looking deathly pale, shocked, and frightened as he stood near his car—was softly answering questions directed at him by one of our fellow cops.

We started interviewing witnesses, as sensitively and discreetly as possible, given the circumstances, and details of the accident started to emerge.

"The little thing ran out from between those two parked cars," one older eyewitness told us, pointing to two sedans about midway up the block.

"She was running home to her mama," a young woman told us. "The terrible thing is, her mama witnessed the whole thing from

137

her second-story window. No mother should have to see something that terrible."

John and I asked every eyewitness the same questions, trying to get the most accurate, consistent narrative as to what had happened. Two questions we asked everyone were, *Was the driver speeding?* and *Did it appear he saw the little girl before hitting her?*

To a person, the witnesses responded "No" to both questions.

Then other horrifying details came out.

"The right front of the vehicle struck the child," one witness told us. "That knocked her down. And, before the driver could stop, she was run over by both the right front and right rear tires."

Amid all the chaos at the accident scene, the crowd continued to wail, and suddenly I became aware of the mother's voice rising above everyone else's.

"This was my fault! Oh, my Lord, this was my fault!" she wailed pitifully. "I'd just called to her to 'come home right away,' and that child was just obeying me!"

We concluded the driver was a victim in this accident, just like the child and her mother. Based on our investigation, we believed he'd violated no laws. He was released to go home and deal with the horror of that afternoon.

After we finished at the scene, we headed to M.E.H. to check on the condition of the little girl. But en route we received the terrible news that she had died.

The coroner's deputies were awaiting our arrival at the hospital. We were greeted by the deputy coroner and taken to an off-limits viewing room, where the body was detained prior to transfer to the morgue.

I'll never forget what I saw in there. It kept me awake many nights over the following years, since I had children of my own, at the time, who were close in age to the victim.

The room was stark white and contained only the table on which lay the body. The little girl was slightly built and pretty. At first glance, she looked as though she were merely sleeping; there didn't appear to be any trauma. But when the deputy coroner pulled down the sheet, we immediately saw the tire tread prints, like a ragged sash across her chest and legs. She didn't have a chance.

Several weeks later, a coroner's inquest was held. He ruled the death was accidental, and no charges would be filed. After the hearing, the child's family came over to Bill and me and thanked us for the way the case was handled. They said they were grateful for the dignity extended to the family by all of us involved.

The Squeal and the Siren

My partner at this time was an officer named Ed Fagalde. Ed had a sort of fatherly, Gomer Pyle-like quality about him. Handsome, white-haired, and about fifty, he was very folksy, gregarious, and likeable—and kind of a ham. Like Jackie Gleason's character in *The Honeymooners*, Ed always seemed to be working on some amusing get-rich-quick scheme. Or he'd relentlessly bet with fellow officers on upcoming ballgames or other such harmless things.

One of Ed's favorite things to do was to walk into a neighborhood bar called the Inn-Justice, engage in conversation with myself and fellow officers, and secretly count the number of bottles behind the bar. (Ed had great eyesight and could count the bottles very quickly.) Then he'd suddenly turn to someone and say, "You know, I bet you I can tell you *exactly* how many bottles are behind that bar." I saw a fair number of people fall for the scheme, and Ed would walk away with some easy money. But it was all in good fun; just silly adult games.

One night, around 7 p.m. on a particularly stormy and rainy night, Ed and I were working the 3 to 11 p.m. tour in the traffic 3 car. Suddenly we got an urgent call:

"Traffic 3 . . . 2nd and Harrison . . . a 519 (injury accident) . . . ambulances en route . . . fire department vehicle involved . . . respond Code 2 (red light with caution – no siren)."

Upon arrival at the scene, we found what appeared to be two large vehicles, tangled up and engulfed in enormous, violently dancing flames. The flames were shooting high into the night. Quickly we were able to determine that one vehicle was a fire truck—a hook and ladder—and the other was a livestock truck. The fire department was working feverishly to extinguish the fire.

We immediately were advised there was a fireman lost somewhere in the debris. He was manning the tiller on the hook

141

and ladder, and apparently was knocked off upon impact. As if that weren't enough, the livestock truck was loaded with pigs—many of which had been rocked free by the collision. The trailer was on its side and we saw pigs scampering all around, all over the crash site. Four or five other pigs were hideously burning, having been covered by fuel spilling from the truck. Upon seeing the wretched animals burning alive, one of the motorcycle cops at the scene took it upon himself to pull out his weapon and end the pigs' agony. It was the right thing to do under the circumstances. And the livestock company agreed.

Unfortunately, the fireman was found too late; he was burned to death beneath the fire truck. He died instantly upon impact, the coroner ruled. Other injuries at the scene were mostly minor.

After several hours of investigation, we were able to piece together what happened:

The fire truck was speeding up 2nd Street answering a fire alarm. Its red light was flashing and siren wailing in the stormy night. At the same time, the hog truck was emerging off the San Francisco Bay Bridge on Harrison Street. Just as the light turned green for the hog truck, the fire truck barreled through the intersection against the red light. But it had the right-of-way because of the Code 3 (red-light and siren) circumstances. Moments later the deadly crash ensued.

When I later asked the hog-truck driver to tell me what happened, he said, "I just couldn't hear the siren because of the squeals coming from the pigs in the trailer. And I couldn't see the fire truck's flashing red lights, because of all this heavy rain."

We determined the driver was not at fault. It was just a sad, tragic accident—one that cost a San Francisco firefighter his life.

San Francisco lost a brave man that night, and his family lost a loving husband and father.

We Were Lucky

During the 1960s, many American cities experienced racial tension that blew up into full-scale riots. San Francisco was no exception. Starting on September 27, 1966, a race riot gripped Hunters Point, a black neighborhood, after a white police officer shot and killed a seventeen-year-old African-American as he fled the scene of a stolen car.

For several days, Hunters Point looked like a scene from an apocalyptic war movie. Danger and chaos gripped the sector, and open warfare raged between the African-American community and the "establishment."

In this case, the "establishment" mostly meant us—cops.

We became the key targets of the violence, although other targets included firemen, emergency medical technicians, and even military personnel assigned to bases around San Francisco. The rioters were so brazen and fearless that the U.S. Marines on security duty at the gates of Hunters Point Naval Station were under small-arms attack for several days. We police officers and our families even received anonymous, threatening phone calls at our homes. My wife Priscilla received numerous calls while I was working the late-night shift, in which the caller would say things like, "We know where you and your family live."

The situation got so explosive and Third World-like that the fire department could not respond to calls in the Hunters Point projects without being accompanied by police riding shotgun. Potrero Station police cruisers would not respond unless they had backup.

One evening during this time, while on patrol in the car dubbed Traffic 4, Bill and I received a call to respond to a location in the center of the Hunters Point projects. It was around 7 p.m.

"Traffic 4 . . . Traffic 4," the radio dispatcher called above the static, "Respond to 519 (injury accident . . . ambulance on the way)."

He gave us the location, and Bill and I warily shot glances at each other as Bill hammered down the accelerator. We knew cruising into Hunters Point could be a death sentence.

But we didn't know the half of it.

As we passed several cop cars en route, officers in those cars looked at us like we were stark-raving mad.

And they had good reason to.

What we didn't realize was, we had been incorrectly placed on a different radio channel from the regular patrol cars, and hadn't heard about the latest—and worst—explosion of the riots.

As soon as we arrived, we knew we were in big trouble. The street lights had all been smashed out, and the small shopping center was enveloped in a deep, dangerous darkness. It felt like we had entered the gates of Hell.

Suddenly—without warning—our cruiser was surrounded by two hundred violently-angry, screaming people carrying sticks, bats, and other makeshift weapons. It was as if they had appeared from nowhere. Or from the pits of Hell.

Our hands shot out to lock our doors, and we un-holstered our sidearms. I grabbed our shotgun, then ripped the radio off its stand, as the rioters began to violently rock our patrol car.

"Traffic 4 calling . . . Traffic 4!" I shouted above the violent frenzy. "Officers being attacked by rioters! Request backup! Request backup!"

Fists slammed against our windows and the car violently lurched back and forth as the rioters attempted to turn us over. All I could see was a violent kaleidoscope of angry faces, open mouths hurling curses at us, fists pumping at us defiantly and trying to smash in the windows.

As the chaos raged, I remember one clear thought coming into my head. I spoke it aloud to Bill: "If we go, we're taking some of these SOBs with us!"

"Hold on, Ray!" Bill yelled back at me, above the murderous fray. The car lurched violently close to the tipping point. "I'll get us the hell out of here!"

The car plunged back upright and, just as it did, Bill gunned the accelerator. Luckily, our tires grabbed earth and the car shot forward, nearly running over several of the rioters in front of us. My hand lashed out to turn on the red lights and siren, and they came screamingly alive as we peeled ourselves away from the murderous crowd.

As soon as we were out of danger, I grabbed the radio and called in.

"What the *hell* is going on?" I yelled into the mouthpiece. "We could have been killed!"

"Race riots have again exploded across Hunters Point," came the response. "Worst outbreak yet . . . reports of mass rioting, bedlam, chaos . . . stores being looted."

There was a pause and then the dispatcher said, "Traffic 4 . . . my sincere apology for putting you on the wrong channel before . . . for not letting you know."

Bill and I looked at each other, shaking our heads. Bill looked like he'd seen a ghost, and I'm sure I looked just as bad.

"Jeez," Bill muttered. "I guess now we know why those Potrero cops looked at us like we were nuts when we responded to *that* call."

The riot ultimately lasted 128 hours and was only quelled when Mayor Shelley called in the National Guard.

Officer, Can You Give Me a Hand?

Bill and I were working the 2 to 10 p.m. watch, assigned to Traffic 2. A call came in, alerting us that an inspector's unit wanted some help (*not* a 406) at 8th and Market Streets, at the Del Webb Hotel. We were only six blocks away, so we quickly responded to the call.

Minutes later, upon our arrival, we found ourselves in the esteemed presence of the all-time super-sleuth, the man known far and wide as "Inspector Yas." His real name was Stanislas Yasiniski. He was grateful to see us, and immediately filled us in on the details of the case.

"I and several other plainclothes inspectors and officers have been working this hotel detail," Yas said in his thick Eastern European accent. "There's been a rash of hotel burglaries, and we're trying our damnest to knock that number down."

He continued: "While I was wandering around the hotel lobby this afternoon—doing my best not to look like a cop—I was asked by a guest, or someone I thought was a guest, for a favor. He was pushing a valet cart loaded with clothes through the lobby, and he asked if I'd help him get it out the front door, into his van."

"Well," Yas said, smiling painfully as he began turning red as a beet, "as you boys know, I never can refuse a citizen in need. So I helped him push the cart down 8th Street, to his parked van. We loaded up the van, and I told him I'd return the cart to the hotel."

About thirty minutes later, Yas said, he got the egg-on-your-face news.

"Hotel security was contacted by a commercial tenant, owner of a dress shop on the main floor, to report they'd been robbed," Yas said, looking chagrined. "The dress shop was in the process of receiving a shipment of ladies' dresses, which were hanging on a valet cart just outside the store's lobby entrance."

When hotel management informed Yas of the robbery, even *he* was able to put two and two together:

The "hotel guest"—the one Yas just had helped—was, in fact, the thief.

And Inspector Yas had just helped him make a clean get-away!

"So . . . um . . . can you boys help me search the area for the van—and keep this whole thing mum?"

Loyalty to a fellow law-enforcement officer—one of the Keystone Cops variety, in this case—kicked in, and Bill and I never said squat about the incident.

The suspect was not apprehended that day, and I'm not sure if he ever was. But Inspector Yas kept his dignity—such as it was—and was forever grateful.

Fatal Errand

It was a Saturday afternoon and I was working solo out of the AIB (Accident Investigation Bureau) in "Traffic 2" (my radio call number).

Suddenly, my peaceful patrol was interrupted by an urgent call:

"Traffic 2 . . . 8th and Harrison . . . a 519 (injury accident) . . . possibly fatal . . . ambulance rolling."

Immediately I shot back, "10-4," gunned the accelerator, and sped toward the scene of the accident. I was in the southwest part of the city, so it took me ten or fifteen minutes to get there.

When I arrived on the scene, I immediately took in the sights and sounds of a devastating crash site. People from the neighborhood, along with newspaper and television reporters, were milling on the sidewalk—talking, yelling—as they gawked at the mangled wreckage of a Greyhound Bus and a sedan. The sedan's victims already had been transported to Mission Emergency Hospital, and the brutal accident scene was being preserved by the solo motorcycle officers sent to control the traffic flow.

What I was about to learn was even more devastating than the accident itself.

Within moments, I learned the sedan was an unmarked police car, assigned to the Bureau of Inspectors. That meant the victim or victims were members of the San Francisco Police Department.

I felt a tense knot in my stomach as I searched for the identities of the victims. Following department procedure, I requested a Superior officer "904" (meet) me at the scene. I asked the other officer to try to locate additional eye witnesses. Then I began to check out the vehicles involved.

It was a horrifying, grisly site. The unmarked police car was completely caved in on the middle of its right side. Blood was spattered everywhere in the car's interior. The windshield, rearview mirror, and windshield frame were bent to form a huge, lethally pointed V-shape. Hanging hideously from this spear-like object was blood-red brain matter.

Backing away from the shocking site, I radioed in.

"What is the condition of the victim or victims at the hospital?" I asked.

Initially, there was no clear, definitive information they could relay. So I immediately went back to my examination of the crash site. I began checking the condition of the Greyhound passengers. Most were okay, and none had sustained anything beyond minor injuries. They were either treated at the scene or taken to the emergency hospital for further check-up.

Later, when I went to the hospital to check on the condition of the unknown victims, I received terrible news.

"Two confirmed fatalities," I was told. "One male, one female. Died instantly upon impact."

Then—before long—I was told the identity of the victims.

My heart dropped.

I was told one victim was Inspector Jim Johnson (a pseudonym).

And the other victim was Jim's wife.

I retained a mask of composure on the outside, but inside I was reeling. This wasn't just a terrible loss of human life; it was a personal loss. I knew the Johnsons very well.

Jim had been with the police force for years. He was in his mid-forties (about ten years older than me at the time), athletic and friendly. He had a great sense of humor and a wonderful family. My boys and daughter were active in things like Pop Warner Football, and so were Jim's kids. He always acted very happy to see me and my wife, Priscilla. We'd always been very fond of him.

Jim's wife was wonderful, too. She was attractive and outgoing, and always very supportive of her husband and of community events in Marin County.

Now came the sad task of trying to piece together why they'd died.

We knew, of course, they'd been killed when a Greyhound bus torpedoed into the side of their car.

But why were they there?

What was Jim's wife doing in the unmarked police car with him?

As I interviewed eye witnesses, several stated that Jim's car had run the red light.

Why had Jim done that? What circumstances set that up?

It was crucial for all concerned that we get the facts straight and absolutely rock-solid, because Jim's pension—and thus the future of his children—was at stake. And the fact that it had been an accident between a San Francisco police officer and a major corporation such as Greyhound Bus made my report especially challenging. So my attitude was: *Don't rush the report. Make sure all your "i's" are dotted and your "t's" crossed.* Part of the way I did that was to have my fellow investigating officers actively search for additional eye witnesses, which proved fruitful.

After days of intense investigation and interviews—including listening to tapes of police radio calls around the time of the accident—we determined Inspector Jim Johnson was responding to an urgent call about a hold-up in-progress, several blocks from the scene of the accident.

That's why Jim had been traveling at such a high rate of speed down Harrison Avenue.

That's why he'd run the red light at 8th and Harrison.

That's why the Greyhound had so brutally T-boned his car.

But there was one final mystery:

Why was Jim's wife with him in the unmarked police car?

It turns out, Jim's wife worked at the Emporium on Market Street on Saturdays, and Jim had picked her up to take her home. He was headed to the Hall of Justice to turn in his car and pick up his own car when he decided to roll in on the hold-up call.

It was a fateful decision.

Inspector Johnson's pension was awarded to his surviving children since his death was considered job-related.

I will never forget that Saturday afternoon.

Fred – Former Partner – S Squad

Fred (a pseudonym) was in his late thirties. He was a nice, generous man—the son of Yugoslavian immigrants—and was a good friend to a lot of people. He had been in the police department more than twelve years, and had worked both uniform and plain clothes.

As so often happens in police work, one day—out of the blue—Fred's world turned upside down, never to be the same.

Here's what happened:

As Fred was apprehending and arresting a suspect, the suspect stuck a German Luger in Fred's stomach and fired—but the gun didn't go off.

The suspect was arrested without further incident. But months later—in a delayed reaction to the horror and stress he felt from that incident—Fred began experiencing a form of Post Traumatic Stress Disorder. It became so bad he eventually received a job-related retirement pension.

During his recovery period, Fred spent a great deal of time in the psych ward. I was one of the only people allowed to visit him and, in fact, occasionally was able to take him out for some fresh air and dinner.

Fred had two daughters who dearly loved him, but the same—sadly—could not be said of his spoiled-brat, wanna-be-glamour-girl wife, Alice (a pseudonym). She was a mean, demanding person, who never overlooked an opportunity to belittle him. She was from a very wealthy family, and never let Fred forget it. She constantly put him down for only bringing in a cop's salary.

"Alice the Shrew" became legendary—at least in our circles—one night during a cocktail party at the International Hotel in Las Vegas, which included representatives from police departments all over the country.

Everything was going fine and dandy, when suddenly the atmosphere in the room turned tense. The next thing we knew,

Alice had done her best Muhammad Ali impression, and decked the executive vice-president of a major insurance company.

That's right—she landed a punch on the guy's jaw that put him instantly on the "canvas" (an expensive rug, in this case).

The hapless victim—and his famous insurance company—were doing business with police associations all over the country. But that didn't deter Alice one second. She claimed he had made a pass at her, and, at first, she'd slapped him. He was so furious and offended by her actions that he attempted to retaliate—and ended up putting his fist through the wall.

That's when Alice decked him.

Anyone who knew Alice wasn't really surprised.

They *were* surprised that Fred stayed with such a mean, unsupportive woman.

But by that time, life had taken its toll on Fred, and he probably stayed with Alice out of world-weariness, and love for his daughters.

Where to Eat

During each daily shift, one of the crucial things cops must sort out is the answer to that all-important question: *Where do we eat?*

Since we were San Francisco police officers, we were like kids in a candy store. (Forgive me for being biased, but I think San Francisco is the Culinary Capitol of the U.S.)

But unfortunately, there was an unofficial protocol we had to follow, which severely limited our on-duty choices. One of the crucial considerations, for example, was how "cop-friendly" the restaurant was.

One place that passed that test with flying colors was Mead's Cafeteria, which—believe it or not—was in Skid Row. Although you would certainly see drunks in there from time to time, the place was super-clean, the food was good, the owner loved cops, and we could (usually) eat without being disturbed. If a problem arose, the owner would handle it himself.

One evening I witnessed a perfect example of this:

Bill and I were in Mead's having dinner. Suddenly, a man sitting a couple of tables away did a swan dive into his soup bowl.

Landed head first, he did.

He was obviously drunk as hell . . . and had passed out with spoon poised and at the ready.

"Ray, looks like we better—", Bill started to say, pointing at the guy. Just then the owner—who looked exactly like Mr. Clean—came dashing from behind the counter.

"Gentlemen, please finish your meals!" he said. "I can handle this. No need to concern yourselves!"

With that, the owner grabbed the patron by the back of his collar, dragged him out of the cafeteria, and propped him up against a nearby fire hydrant.

"You're no longer welcome at Mead's!" we heard the owner yell to the drunk outside.

155

Moments later, he came back through the front door and immediately made a beeline for our table.

"My sincere apologies, gentlemen. I hope your dinner was not unduly disturbed."

That sort of treatment was a great perk of the job. Most places like to have uniformed police officers in their place of business as a security measure, treat you like family, and often express their gratitude by offering to "comp" your meal. (We technically weren't supposed to accept complimentary meals, but, I assure you, that policy was regularly disregarded.)

We Didn't Know
Jake Needed Help

It may seem like an over-statement to some people, but in my experience it's true: Generally speaking, police officers are like time bombs. They can go off at any time. The intense stress that comes with the job—that builds and builds over years and years—does that to them.

Jake Gibson was one of its casualties.

Jake was a fine cop: quiet, gentle, funny, and competent. He liked to joke around with people, and he struck people as happy-go-lucky, although no one—except possibly his police partner Steve Harrison—seemed to know him very well. But everyone liked him. He was a veteran of more than twenty years in the Department, married and with a family.

Then it happened.

It was around 9:45 p.m., and the 2 to 10 p.m. watch was just ending our tour of duty. We were finishing up our paperwork in the Accident Investigation Bureau business office at the Hall of Justice. Some of the crews started to head downstairs to the locker room to change into street clothes. The rest of the guys were just hanging out until the watch commander reported us off-duty.

Suddenly I heard a loud, hideous explosion. It sounded like it came from downstairs. Everyone started running chaotically downstairs toward the locker room.

Within seconds, Steve Harrison came running from the locker room, screaming that Jake had just shot himself with his .357 magnum. Steve looked absolutely shattered—pale and shocked. He had spent years with his partner, Jake. They were like brothers.

An ambulance was called, but there was nothing anyone could do. Jake's head was spattered against the wall. He had gone downstairs to "eat his gun."

We were all absolutely devastated. This couldn't happen to one of the good guys. And Jake was a good guy.

As it turned out, although Jake Gibson had seemed like a happy-go-lucky, joking kind of guy, that was the mask he showed the world. There was much going on inside him we failed to see.

Had Jake shown any signs of distress? If so, *why had we missed them?*

That was one of the hardest things for us to deal with: We helped strangers on a daily basis, but we couldn't help one of our own.

Over the years people have asked me, "Why did Jake choose to commit suicide in the police department? Why that specific setting?"

I believe he was making a statement. He was tired of the rat race. He was tired and spent by the endless, withering stress of police work.

Jake Gibson was buried with full department protocol. His death was determined to be job-related, thereby protecting the insurance benefits available to his family.

Too Close to Home

My Uncle Frank O'Brien, my mother's brother, was an alcoholic. He was a sweet man; very well-liked and a wonderful storyteller. Being Irish—all Irish—he liked people and made friends easily. Before alcoholism began getting the better of him, he was a hard-working chemist for Eureka Fluids, which made embalming fluid. He also worked for a while for Sunshine Raisins, during which time he'd occasionally send me big bags of raisins. I loved raisins, so that made Uncle Frank quite popular with me.

When I was very little, I'd hear stories about Uncle Frank, but never met him until I was about seven. Even at that age, I saw he would give the shirt off his back to help people. But because of his drinking problem, he needed help himself.

I grew up watching my mother respond to Uncle Frank's cries for help—and sometimes saw my parents arguing over it. My mother would meet Uncle Frank once or twice a week, on street corners or in bars, to give him food, clothing, sometimes money, and always her love and support. This would sometimes lead to flare-ups between my mother and father.

"I don't want you bringing food out to him!" my father would yell. "He's just a bum!" He implied that—to use today's language—my mother was simply enabling Uncle Frank, and my father had no sympathy or patience for that.

On very rare occasions, Uncle Frank would be invited to our house for Sunday dinner, or for another special meal. I always looked forward to it because he was so sweet-tempered and such a wonderful storyteller. But it made for awkward table conversation. Many family members, gathered around the table, wouldn't talk to Uncle Frank. Even his own brother, my Uncle Ray, the police officer, would have nothing to do with him. I never knew the reason other than often hearing Uncle Ray, like my father, call Uncle Frank "just a bum." I understood later that Uncle Frank had shown up drunk at several family get-togethers, and my father didn't want his children seeing that.

When I became a police officer and was exposed to the world of alcoholism and its victims, I could not help but understand the heartache of having a loved one with that illness. Sometimes there seemed to be nothing anyone could do to help these unfortunate, sick people. I knew deep in my heart my uncle's situation was not going to end well.

For a number of years, after I joined the police force, Uncle Frank would be picked up on the street, dead drunk, by my fellow police officers. Many of them knew who he was, and treated him kindly out of respect for me.

One afternoon, just after going on duty, I received a radio call directing me to call my office (a 901 call). I responded and the station-duty officer said, "Ray, there's a message here for you. You need to call your mother. It's apparently something to do with your uncle. Please call your mother right away."

I thought this odd since this was the first time in many years that my mother had called me at work.

When I returned my mother's call, she was terribly distraught and crying and told me, "I just received a call from the San Francisco coroner's office. They told me they've recovered what they believe to be the remains of Uncle Frank. They requested that I come to the coroner's office to make a positive identification. I just can't do that, Ray. I just can't face doing that. Can you please do it?" she asked me through her tears. I told her of course I would.

Because of my assignment, the Accident Bureau, I had a pretty good relationship with the coroner's office, since there are so many fatal accidents in San Francisco in any given year. But in this case, the professional courtesy extended to me was more than I bargained for. When I explained the situation to the deputy coroner on duty that day, he expressed his sympathy and said he would help me. I went to the coroner's office and one of the investigating officers said to me gently, "This is going to be rough for you to see, Ray. Really, really rough."

I was taken to the receiving room and an autopsy table was rolled out. There was a body on the table covered by a white sheet. Before the sheet was removed, the deputy coroner explained that the body had been found in a fleabag hotel room. The person had died in bed and had been dead for several days.

"It's not a pretty sight," the deputy said. Then he removed the sheet.

Nothing I had ever experienced prepared me for what I saw (gory details purposely excluded). The body was shockingly decomposed. But after a bit, and with some help, I was able to make the necessary, albeit sad, positive identification of Uncle Frank.

I got in touch with my mother and advised her that, yes, it was Uncle Frank. She seemed to be at peace with that, knowing her brother no doubt was in a better place. She whispered before I hung up, "Now he no longer has to suffer."

Complacency
(Time to Hang It Up)

Bill and I were heading west on 16th Street near Mission Street at about 6:15 p.m. We were assigned to the Traffic 3 radio car. It was getting near dinnertime and we were discussing where we may take 10-7M (meal break) when we were interrupted by an urgent radio message:

"All cars . . . any Mission cars . . . a hot prowl at 619 Guerrero . . . Apartment 312."

My experience had been that these calls often amounted to nothing. They might simply be triggered by a husband and wife arguing louder than their neighbors appreciated.

But Bill and I looked at each other and I said, "What the hell. Let's go on the call. Then we'll take 10-7M."

I picked up the radio and shot back, "10-4 . . . Traffic 3 is rolling . . . We'll take the back of the building."

Bill pulled into the garage area behind the three-story apartment building and parked the car. A few minutes went by and the call was not Code 4'rd (canceled), which is what usually happens with this type of call. So I told Bill I was going to check it out.

I leaped out of the cruiser and started to make my way up the back stairway. My flashlight was in my right hand and my .357 magnum was in its holster.

Because of personal things going on with me at the time, I was not properly focused on what I was doing. I was seriously thinking of resigning from the police department. The stress had been "way too much for way too long," and I was deeply frustrated by the criminal justice bureaucracy. I was sick to death of a system I viewed as way too soft on crime, constantly springing hardened criminals back onto the streets, which victimized both the public and the police force. I was the father of three by this point, and found myself constantly asking myself, *Why do I need this? There's no future in this.* As a result, I had become quite complacent.

And on this particular day, that complacency nearly cost me my life.

As I turned up the third flight of stairs, a male voice directed at me suddenly rang out.

"You're dead, cop!!!" the voice screamed and—in the next second—I saw a huge handgun pointed directly down at me. In the same split-second, the door behind the gunman shot open, and I saw the outline of the suspect training his gun at me.

I had absolutely no time to react. No time to go for my gun. No room to jump out of the way.

I thought I'd bought the farm.

Suddenly, there appeared in the doorway an officer (Bob Quinn) from the Mission Station. Bob thrust his gun at the suspect's right temple and yelled, *"Drop your gun!!! Put up your hands!!!"* Bob Quinn had a John Wayne vibe about him. He spoke with a Texas accent and people knew he meant business.

I immediately raced up the stairs and helped Bob cuff the suspect.

"Thank you, man," I grunted at Bob. "You . . . you saved my life."

Then we transported the suspect to the Mission Station for booking.

Later, I went to talk with the suspect in his holding cell. My curiosity had gotten the better of me.

"Do you recognize me?" I asked.

"Yeah," he grunted matter-of-factly. "You were the cop standing between me and freedom."

I took that in, and a moment later asked him, "Would you have shot me?"

Without missing a beat, he shot back, "You bet your ass I would've."

As it turned out, the gunman was a two-time loser and we'd caught him in the commission of a felony with a gun. Under California's three-strikes law, that automatically meant life in prison. So he felt he had nothing to lose by shooting me.

When Bill and I finally took our 10-7M, I said to Bill, "I'm lucky I'm still alive. I've been complacent lately, and there's zero room for complacency in this business. It almost cost me my life—and maybe someone else's. I think it's time for me to hang it up."

AFTERMATH

Tragedy of the Small-Town Cop

In 2001, Priscilla and I moved to a small, suburban town near Nashville, Tennessee. Music had always played a large part in Priscilla's life and, in the 1980s, she began forming business relationships in the Nashville music community. So, by the time we made the decision to move from California to Tennessee, we already enjoyed many warm friendships with people in the Nashville area.

Although I enjoyed living near Nashville (and still do), I found myself missing my old connections to law enforcement. After asking around a bit and otherwise networking, I soon found myself invited to become active in the local Crime Stoppers organization, eventually becoming a member of its board. In this role I quickly made new acquaintances who, like myself, had an affinity for police officers and their work.

That's how I met John (a pseudonym), a fifty-year-old police officer in the throes of anxiety and depression. John was in a genuine panic over his upcoming retirement from the local police department. He'd been a cop for nearly twenty-five years.

My house was part of the area John patrolled most days, and he would often stop in to talk with me while he was on break, or before or after his shift. My house became something of a haven for him. We would sit together—often on a daily basis—and talk. I began to feel truly bad for this man. As his retirement date drew nearer and nearer, he became more and more despondent at the thought of leaving the police force, at the thought of retiring to civilian life. He believed his life would be over.

From the first day we met, John started "unloading" on me in this manner—which he desperately needed to do—telling me of various things that had happened to him during his many years as a small-town cop. Luckily, I'm pretty talkative, so we had long, deep conversations about his situation.

169

As I got to know John better, he opened up more and more. The major theme of most of what he told me was that he didn't feel adequate as a human being without his uniform on. He told me again and again that the thought of being without his uniform—being just an average citizen—terrified him.

During this time, John kept asking me, "Are you sure it's okay for me to drop by like this?" (By then he was doing so literally every day, sometimes twice a day.) I, of course, reassured him it was.

"I don't have any skills, Ray, aside from police work," he once told me. "I don't know how I'm going to fit into the world if I'm not wearing a badge."

"I know things are rough now," I would tell him. "But the world is your oyster. All the incredible experience you've had as a police officer—for these twenty-plus years—will serve you handsomely. I guarantee it. As a matter of fact, I bet you'll eventually wonder why you didn't leave police work sooner." He would look at me when I said things like that, but I couldn't tell if I was making much headway with him.

"I'll be honest with you, John," I'd continue, "it's frustrating for me to listen to you. Simply because I know you've got such potential. You've just got to go out and look around. Ask yourself, *What do I really want to do? What do I have an appetite for?*

So I started using that kind of approach, stressing to him how valuable his experience would be to an employer in the "civilian world." His ability to deal with people . . . his decision-making ability . . . if you looked at it from an employer's perspective, those things would be incredibly valuable.

But I mostly listened to him, and tried to be his friend. I repeatedly told him, "What you are—what you represent—is something to be very proud of."

But still he seemed to maintain that lost, desperate feeling. It was a feeling I could understand. I'd felt that way during my last months on the police force. As things went on, I heard through a mutual friend that John had said, "I really respect Ray. I can talk to him." I hoped my "being there" for him was having a positive impact.

Then—one Sunday night—things suddenly took a negative turn.

Priscilla and I were away from home, visiting family in Knoxville, and I heard that John had stopped by our house. Even though he came by frequently, this was very unusual. He had never dropped by on a Sunday night before.

Suddenly I began to get a queasy feeling about things—call it a cop's sixth sense.

As soon as I returned home, I called Peter Bryant (a pseudonym), the former cop who had initially introduced me to John. I told Peter, "I think there's something really wrong with John. More than we knew."

Early the following Sunday morning, John called me and asked if he could drop by. I said, "sure" and, not long after, he was in my house again. He looked very agitated, very distraught. His eyes were filled with tears.

We had our visit—I did my best to console him—and then he went on his way. I didn't tell him how I would spend the rest of the day.

That afternoon, Priscilla and I took a long drive out in the country surrounding Nashville. By the time we got home, it was already dark out. Almost as soon as we entered our home, the phone rang.

"Ray, I have terrible news," Peter said. "John is dead."

I was stunned—shocked—but managed to ask, "How?" I was thinking he must have been killed in an auto accident or something.

"He shot himself," Peter said.

I attended the wake a few days later.

I'll always believe John made his decision weeks before actually carrying it out. My gut feeling is he had gotten to the point where he desperately needed someone to walk him through that transition in his life, to tell him things would be okay. People around him had done their best to do that, but his despair overwhelmed him.

There but for the grace of God go many.

* * *

There is one final thing I'd like to mention about John.

About six months before his death, I shared with him rough drafts of several of the stories that now appear in *406: Officer Needs Assistance*. He read them with keen interest and, in fact, even sent me a page-long, handwritten note about them. He wrote, in part:

> *Ray,*
>
> *[These are] wonderful and exciting, although sometimes tragic, stories. [I noted in them] honesty, sincerity, an entertaining quality, and a missing of the "star." Once you have been a cop, you will carry that with you the rest of your life—the power to enforce, a heart to forgive, the loss that you deal with, whether it be one of your own or the ordinary man or woman. All are God's children.*
>
> *[No matter] how you looked at things in your stories— thanks only to a wonderful, loving God—survival was the answer.*
>
> *John*

I think often of John. When I think of "officer needs assistance," I see a kaleidoscope of faces, and John's is always one of them.

Rest in peace, my friend.

Epilogue

I characterize my experience as a police officer as probably the very best training ground a person could ever have. The opportunity to make a better person out of oneself was freely offered to everyone who graduated from the police academy. It was a peak-experience education.

The people you run into while working as a cop represent a broad-brush landscape. The over-all experience—and having the opportunity to deal with such a huge cross-section of humanity—gave us the opportunity to develop confidence and the ability to communicate with our peers and our "employer," the citizens of San Francisco. No conventional desk job I could have taken in the corporate world would have given me even a glimmer of what I experienced as a San Francisco cop. It was the most well-rounded, character-building occupation I ever could have hoped for.

As I mentioned at the beginning of this book, I started in the police force as a very young, idealistic man of twenty-one. Over the arc of the next decade, I gradually saw my youthful idealism fade, as real-world realities kicked in. I began encountering things that made me disillusioned with the system, with the way law enforcement work was carried out. After you repeatedly are forced to deal with soft-on-crime judges, and soft-on-crime juvenile-court "referees," the disillusionment begins to sink in in a way that taints nearly everything in your life.

One particular experience brought this home more forcibly than anything else I ever lived through. Here's what happened:

An elderly couple from Sacramento got lost as they drove into San Francisco. They were trying to find Candlestick Park and the Giants baseball game, but, because they didn't know their way around, they ended up in a rough housing project in Hunters Point, more than a mile from their destination.

It was a hot summer's night, and there were lots of people outside, milling about outside a neighborhood bar.

That's when things suddenly turned dark and deadly.

Evidently, when the couple slowed to ask directions, they were violently T-boned by another car. Their car was struck so violently it rolled over. Then the car that T-boned them backed up and left the scene—a felony hit-and-run.

But soon things got even worse.

Rather than help the elderly couple, several neighborhood thugs approached the couple's car, threw open the doors, and starting violently attacking them. Within seconds, the elderly man and woman were soaked in their own blood, shocked and dazed and wondering what they'd done to provoke such a vicious attack. And their wallets were gone, too.

Seconds later, my dashboard lit up with an urgent dispatch. My partner and I were told to race to the scene of the crime—and to expect to find "hostile witnesses" there. What we didn't know at the time was that these "hostile witnesses" were, in fact, the very thugs who had savagely attacked the elderly couple.

As soon as I arrived, I encountered an unmistakable vibe from the people milling about the accident. It felt like *Get the hell out of here. This is our neighborhood. You cops don't belong here.* (This was not long after the Hunters Point riots.)

Once we and other policemen were on the scene, the couple finally had someone to help them. They were rushed to Mission Emergency Hospital, where doctors saw—as we had—the woman's badly smashed face and her severely broken jaw. She and her husband were still soaked in blood.

After conducting our investigation, we talked to the District Attorney about the case. We stressed to him how horrifying this attack had been, how long-term the effects likely would be. (Even six months later, the woman was barely able to talk, her jaw had been so violently shattered.)

A major problem was, though, that all the witnesses to both crimes—the felony hit-and-run and the subsequent beating of the couple—were hostile. None of them wanted to help the police in the investigation. But we did have the couples' testimony and photos from the crime scene. A subpoena was issued to the four or five hostile witnesses.

Fast forward to the subsequent trial:

My partner and I watched as the elderly couple slowly made their way into the courtroom. We knew we had about ten minutes before the trial would actually begin, so we went over to the District Attorney to talk. He was a young, arrogant guy who wasn't exactly the policeman's best friend either. We quickly went over the police reports with him, after which he told us he was going to the men's room before the trial began. We learned later that all the hostile "witnesses"—whom my partner and I believed actually to be the *assailants*—went to the men's room at the same time.

My partner and I went back to our seats, and watched the District Attorney come back and take his seat. A few minutes later, the judge pounded his gavel, bringing the trial to order.

"Are you prepared to present your case?" the judge asked the D.A.

"I'm not sure," the D.A. responded.

"What do you mean?" the judge asked.

"Well, we have no evidence . . . and no witnesses."

The judge looked at the D.A. with an expression on his face that said, *Then what the heck are we doing here?*

Then he basically *said* that.

I looked at the elderly couple, who looked absolutely stunned.

"Your honor!" the defense attorney shouted, bolting to his feet, "I therefore request that you declare a mistrial!"

The judge nodded, and the next moment his voice filled the chamber. "If that is the case—that we have no evidence and no witnesses—I am, indeed, forced to declare a mistrial."

I could not believe it. Nor could my partner. We shot up out of our seats, and rushed to the D.A.

"What the hell's going on?" we both said in unison.

"There's *no witnesses*," the D.A. shot back at us. (We would discover later—if you can possibly believe this—that the witnesses/assailants had snuck away from the courthouse after going to the men's room.)

The next moment we heard the terrible, anguished wail of the elderly woman, trying her best to say something through her broken jaw. It was absolutely devastating. As she walked by us, out of the courtroom, she was sobbing uncontrollably.

I can't tell you how badly this experience bothered me. I saw, very clearly, that—once again—the system had failed to protect people who were perfectly innocent. It was a horrible miscarriage of justice. And it was the final straw for me.

Four weeks later, I resigned from the police force.

* * *

Why did that incident hit me so hard? Why did I decide—just weeks after that trial—to leave the police force after an entire decade of service?

It had been building for a long time—the sense that the system was soft-on-crime, and stacked against us. Stacked against the cop. I remember sharing conversations with other cops, and the prevailing sentiment at the time was, "This is just not worth it any more. This is not a good job anymore."

The bottom line is: We were participants in the violence and upheaval of the 1960s, in the revolutionary reshuffling of law enforcement. The landscape had changed so dramatically from when I first became a law enforcement officer. San Francisco, and the U.S. as a whole, transformed from a landscape in which the rule of law was respected, to one in which it was not—at least at that time. And if you were the face of law enforcement—the face of the rule of law—you suddenly found yourself outgunned at every turn.

So—for me, at least—it was time to move on. Time to forge a new life.

I became an insurance agent, helping to provide police and other first-responder organizations the protection of insurance services they previously had not been able to access. I'd like to think that Inspector Ray O'Brien, Badge #35—my Uncle Ray— would have been very pleased that I continued to work closely with first responders and their families like that.

* * *

I began this book talking about the deepest, broadest meaning of "officer needs assistance." The phrase, in fact, has many meanings and implications. If you are a police officer, each of these meanings resonates in its own particular way. At first blush, "officer needs assistance" is what we San Francisco police officers meant when we radioed in "406! 406!" It meant we were involved in a complicated—perhaps even dangerous—crime-scene situation and needed other officers to arrive on the scene as back-up. There is an incredible brotherhood among police officers, and, in my experience, each and every one of them was ready, willing, and able to answer that "officer needs assistance" call.

There is also a psychological and emotional implication of "officer needs assistance." A police officer's job is often extremely stressful, and a great strain on his or her psyche. This means the officer needs assistance from their spouse, family, and children. Family members realize the cop's job is among the most dangerous and stressful a person can have, and that it can lead to a lot of emotional baggage. The love, support, and understanding of family members often is one of the cop's greatest motivators. He or she is a human being, after all.

Finally, "officer needs assistance" also carries a deeper meaning in terms of the police officer's role in the community at large. During the writing of this book, police officers regularly were targets of violent aggression from the very people they are sworn to protect. (The incidents in New York City and Ferguson, Missouri are only two in a long list.) Unfortunately, some of this situation seems to be inadvertently driven by the media. They realize they don't sell newspapers by patting police officers on the back. And that's a shame, because assistance from the community is a key component in the police officer's effectiveness and over-all sense of wellbeing.

"Assistance" from the community doesn't have to be something like the local shopkeeper providing a clue that solves a murder mystery. It can be as simple—yet profound—as thanking an officer for his or her service to the community, or acknowledging the debt of gratitude each citizen should feel toward the police. You've probably seen the bumper sticker that reads, "If you're free, thank someone in the military." Perhaps there should be a similar sticker that reads, "If you're safe, thank a cop." Police officers live to earn that kind of appreciation and encouragement from their fellow citizens.

That's one of the important things I wanted to communicate by writing this book.

When you're a police officer, your life is on the line. Your reaction to events can be the make-or-break factor in a situation. And that makes for an extremely stressful life—a life I eventually had to walk away from. But I'll never forget my days as a cop. And I'm happy I was able to share them with you, in the pages of this book.